YOU ARE THE
BELOVED

YOU ARE THE BELOVED

Daily Meditations for
Spiritual Living

BY HENRI J. M. NOUWEN

Compiled and edited by Gabrielle Earnshaw

Convergent
New York

Dedicated to Robert Durback

A Note to the Reader: Generally, the meditations have been drawn from first editions. However, when available, meditations come from revised editions that employ more inclusive language. Some meditations and scriptural passages remain with the language of the Father, based on Henri's understanding of the intimate familiar relationship. All editions used are listed in Works Cited. Other minor changes to the text have been made for clarity.

Copyright © 2017 by The Henri Nouwen Legacy Trust

Published in the United States by Convergent Books, an imprint of the Crown Publishing Group, a division of Penguin Random House LLC, New York. Published in association with Alive Literary Agency, 7680 Goddard Street, Suite 200, Colorado Springs, Colorado, 80920, www.aliveliterary.com.
crownpublishing.com

CONVERGENT BOOKS is a registered trademark and its C colophon is a trademark of Penguin Random House LLC.

For more information about Henri Nouwen, his work, and the work of the Henri Nouwen Society, visit www.HenriNouwen.org.

Library of Congress Cataloging-in-Publication Data is available upon request.

ISBN 978-1-101-90637-8
Ebook ISBN 978-1-101-90638-5

Printed in the United States of America

Book design: Lauren Dong
Jacket design: Jessie Bright
Jacket image: courtesy of Corita Art Center, Immaculate Heart Community

10 9 8 7 6 5 4

First Edition

Introduction

This is a book of daily meditations, selected from the writings, talks, and letters of Henri Nouwen, some of which have never been published before. Taking time for daily meditation was crucial for Henri. It was his time to be present to God, to hear God speak to him.

Reading was an integral part of Henri's daily practice. He had a unique perspective on spiritual reading. In his book *Here and Now,* he wrote:

> Spiritual reading is not only reading about spiritual people or spiritual things. It is also reading spiritually, that is, in a spiritual way! Reading in a spiritual way is reading with a desire to let God come closer to us. . . .
>
> The purpose of spiritual reading . . . is not to master knowledge or information but to let God's Spirit master us. Strange as it may sound, spiritual reading means to let ourselves be read by God! . . .
>
> Spiritual reading is reading with an inner attentiveness to the movement of God's Spirit in our outer and inner lives. With that attentiveness we will allow God to read us and to explain to us what we are truly about.

Henri Nouwen had a lifelong struggle with loneliness and anxiety, which at one point led to a downward spiral of self-rejection and despair. In the depths of his anguish, Henri made a conscious choice to spend a good part of every day in solitude, seeking God. The result was an epiphany: *"You are the Beloved of God."* At first, he could barely hear these words, but gradually he learned to claim them, allowing this primal identity as a child of God to form roots in the soil of his heart. When he recovered, his talks and retreats began to focus more on the immensity of God's compassion and love. In his book *Life of the Beloved,* he wrote:

> All I want to say to you is "You are the Beloved," and all I hope is that you can hear these words as spoken to you with all the tenderness and force that love can hold. My only desire is to make these words reverberate in every corner of your being—"You are the Beloved."

While growing up, Henri heard two contradictory voices in his head about how to live. The first said, "Stay close to the heart of Jesus," and the other cautioned, "Be sure you are successful." Henri was not immune to the call of the secular world, which tells us through subtle and overt ways that we don't quite measure up. We are judged by the amount of money we earn, the number of friends we have, and how productive we are. What Henri heard in the depth of his struggle, however, was counterintuitive and radical—to reject a worldly identity and claim his place as God's Beloved.

In this book, Henri invites us to consider that we, too, are precious in God's sight. So much changes when we do. We become more interested in being than in doing; we bind our wounds rather than run from what causes us pain; we befriend death rather than deny it.

Henri found a new capacity for joy. By claiming his belovedness, he had more compassion for people who hurt him, more courage to live his struggles as gateways to inner freedom. He became more loving, and felt more at peace with himself and the world.

This book of daily meditations is an invitation to walk with Henri Nouwen to the center of your own heart where the soft, gentle voice of God can be heard, *You, too, are the Beloved.*

JANUARY

A New Beginning!

We must learn to live each day, each hour, yes, each min-
ute as a new beginning, as a unique opportunity to make
everything new. Imagine that we could live each moment as
a moment pregnant with new life. Imagine that we could live
each day as a day full of promises. Imagine that we could walk
through the new year always listening to the voice saying to us:
"I have a gift for you and can't wait for you to see it!" Imagine.

Is it possible that our imagination can lead us to the truth
of our lives? Yes, it can! The problem is that we allow our past,
which becomes longer and longer each year, to say to us: "You
know it all; you have seen it all, be realistic; the future will just
be a repeat of the past. Try to survive it as best you can." There
are many cunning foxes jumping on our shoulders and whisper-
ing in our ears the great lie: "There is nothing new under the
sun . . . don't let yourself be fooled."

When we listen to these foxes, they eventually prove themselves right: our new year, our new day, our new hour become
flat, boring, dull, and without anything new.

So what are we to do? First, we must send the foxes back to
where they belong: in their foxholes. And then we must open
our minds and our hearts to the voice that resounds through
the valleys and hills of our life saying: "Let me show you where
I live among my people. My name is 'God-with-you.' I will wipe
all the tears from your eyes; there will be no more death, and
no more mourning or sadness. The world of the past has gone"
(Revelation 21:2–5).

Here and Now

2

Anchor Yourself in God's Love

When Jesus was baptized in the Jordan, he heard a voice from heaven saying, "This is my beloved Son, with whom I am well pleased" (Matthew 3:17). These words revealed the true identity of Jesus as the beloved. Jesus truly heard that voice, and all of his thoughts, words, and actions came forth from his deep knowledge that he was infinitely loved by God. Jesus lived his life from that inner place of love. Although human rejections, jealousies, resentments, and hatred did hurt him deeply, he remained anchored in the love of the Father. At the end of his life, he said to his disciples, "Listen: the time will come—indeed has come already—when you are going to be scattered, each going his own way and leaving me alone. And yet I am not alone, because the Father is with me" (John 16:32).

I know now that the words spoken to Jesus when he was baptized are words spoken also to me and to all who are brothers and sisters of Jesus. My tendencies toward self-rejection and self-deprecation make it hard to hear these words truly and let them descend into the center of my heart. But once I have received these words fully, I am set free from my compulsion to prove myself to the world and can live in it without belonging to it. Once I have accepted the truth that I am God's beloved child, unconditionally loved, I can be sent into the world to speak and to act as Jesus did.

Beyond the Mirror

Your Heart Is the Center of Your Being

In the biblical understanding, our heart is at the center of our being. It's not a muscle, but a symbol for the very center of our being. Now the beautiful thing about the heart is that the heart is the place where we are most ourselves. It is the very core of our being, the spiritual center of our being. Solitude and silence, for instance, are ways to get to the heart, because the heart is the place where God speaks to us, where we hear the voice that calls us beloved. This is precisely the most intimate place. In the famous story, Elijah was standing in front of the cave. God was not in the storm, God was not in the fire and not in the earthquake, but God was in that soft little voice (see 1 Kings 19: 11–12). That soft little voice . . . speaks to the heart. Prayer and solitude are ways to listen to the voice that speaks to our heart, in the center of our being. One of the most amazing things is that if you enter deeper and deeper into that place, you not only meet God, but you meet the whole world there.

Beloved: Henri Nouwen in Conversation

You Are Beloved

Personally, as my struggle reveals, I don't often "feel" like a beloved child of God. But I *know* that that is my most primal identity and I know that I must choose it above and beyond my hesitations.

Strong emotions, self-rejection, and even self-hatred justifiably toss you about, but you are free to respond as you will. You are *not* what others, or even you, think about yourself. You are *not* what you do. You are *not* what you have. You are a full member of the human family, having been known before you were conceived and molded in your mother's womb. In times when you feel bad about yourself, try to choose to remain true to the truth of who you really are. Look in the mirror each day and claim your true identity. Act ahead of your feelings and trust that one day your feelings will match your convictions. Choose now and continue to choose this incredible truth. As a spiritual practice claim and reclaim your primal identity as beloved daughter or son of a personal Creator.

Home Tonight

Know That You Are Welcome

Not being welcome is your greatest fear. It connects with your birth fear, your fear of not being welcome in this life, and your death fear, your fear of not being welcome in the life after this. It is the deep-seated fear that it would have been better if you had not lived.

Here you are facing the core of the spiritual battle. Are you going to give in to the forces of darkness that say you are not welcome in this life, or can you trust the voice of the One who came not to condemn you but to set you free from fear? You have to choose life. At every moment you have to decide to trust the voice that says, "I love you. I knit you together in your mother's womb" (Psalms 139:13).

Everything Jesus is saying to you can be summarized in the words "Know that you are welcome." Jesus offers you his own most intimate life with the Father.

The Inner Voice of Love

Live Under the Blessing

When we lose a family member or friend through death, when we become jobless, when we fail an examination, when we live through a separation or a divorce, when a war breaks out, when an earthquake destroys our home or touches us, the question "Why?" spontaneously emerges. "Why me?" "Why now?" "Why here?" It is so arduous to live without an answer to this "Why?" that we are easily seduced into connecting the events over which we have no control with our conscious or unconscious evaluation. When we have cursed ourselves or allowed others to curse us, it is very tempting to explain all the brokenness we experience as an expression or confirmation of this curse. Before we fully realize it, we have already said to ourselves, "You see, I always thought I was no good. . . . Now I know for sure. The facts of life prove it."

The great spiritual call of the Beloved Children of God is to pull their brokenness away from the shadow of the curse and put it under the light of the blessing. This is not as easy as it sounds. The power of the darkness around us is strong, and our world finds it easier to manipulate self-rejecting people than self-accepting people. But when we keep listening attentively to the voice calling us the Beloved, it becomes possible to live our brokenness, not as a confirmation of our fear that we are worthless, but as an opportunity to purify and deepen the blessing that rests upon us. Physical, mental, or emotional pain lived under the blessing is experienced in ways radically different from physical, mental, or emotional pain lived under the curse.

Life of the Beloved

God Is a Compassionate God

The truly good news is that God is not a distant God, a God to be feared and avoided, a God of revenge, but a God who is moved by our pains and participates in the fullness of the human struggle. . . . God is a compassionate God. This means, first of all, that God is a God who has chosen to be God-with-us. . . . As soon as we call God "God-with-us," we enter into a new relationship of intimacy with him. By calling God Emmanuel, we recognize God's commitment to live in solidarity with us, to share our joys and pains, to defend and protect us, and to suffer all of life with us. The God-with-us is a close God, a God whom we call our refuge, our stronghold, our wisdom, and even, more intimately, our helper, our shepherd, our love. We will never really know God as a compassionate God if we do not understand with our heart and mind that "the Word became flesh and lived among us" (John 1:14).

Compassion

God Needs Me as Much as I Need God

It might sound strange, but God wants to find me as much as, if not more than, I want to find God. Yes, God needs me as much as I need God. God is not the patriarch who stays home, doesn't move, and expects his children to come to him, apologize for their aberrant behavior, beg for forgiveness, and promise to do better. To the contrary, he leaves the house, ignoring his dignity by running toward them, pays no heed to apologies and promises of change, and brings them to the table richly prepared for them.

I am beginning to now see how radically the character of my spiritual journey will change when I no longer think of God as hiding out and making it as difficult as possible for me to find him, but, instead, as the One who is looking for me while I am doing the hiding.

The Return of the Prodigal Son

Surrender Yourself Completely to God's Love

I am growing in the awareness that God wants my whole life, not just part of it. It is not enough to give just so much time and attention to God and keep the rest for myself. It is not enough to pray often and deeply and then move from there to my own projects. . . .

To return to God means to return to God with all that I am and all that I have. I cannot return to God with just half of my being. As I reflected this morning again on the story of the prodigal son and tried to experience myself in the embrace of the father, I suddenly felt a certain resistance to being embraced so fully and totally. I experienced not only a desire to be embraced, but also a fear of losing my independence. I realized that God's love is a jealous love. God wants not just a part of me, but all of me. Only when I surrender myself completely to God's love can I expect to be free from endless distractions, ready to hear the voice of love, and able to recognize my own unique call.

The Road to Daybreak

The Trap of Self-Rejection

Over the years, I have come to realize that the greatest trap in our life is not success, popularity, or power, but self-rejection. Success, popularity, and power can indeed present a great temptation, but their seductive quality often comes from the way they are part of the much larger temptation to self-rejection. When we have come to believe in the voices that call us worthless and unlovable, then success, popularity, and power are easily perceived as attractive solutions. The real trap, however, is self-rejection. . . . As soon as someone accuses me or criticizes me, as soon as I am rejected, left alone, or abandoned, I find myself thinking, "Well, that proves once again that I am a nobody." . . . My dark side says, "I am no good. . . . I deserve to be pushed aside, forgotten, rejected, and abandoned."

Self-rejection is the greatest enemy of the spiritual life because it contradicts the sacred voice that calls us the "Beloved." Being the Beloved constitutes the core truth of our existence.

Life of the Beloved

You Belong to God

At issue here is the question: "To whom do I belong? God or to the world?" Many of my daily preoccupations suggest that I belong more to the world than to God. A little criticism makes me angry, and a little rejection makes me depressed. A little praise raises my spirits, and a little success excites me. It takes very little to raise me up or thrust me down. Often I am like a small boat on the ocean, completely at the mercy of its waves. All the time and energy I spend in keeping some kind of balance and preventing myself from being tipped over and drowning shows that my life is mostly a struggle for survival: not a holy struggle, but an anxious struggle resulting from the mistaken idea that it is the world that defines me. . . .

As long as we belong to this world, we will remain subject to its competitive ways and expect to be rewarded for all the good we do. But when we belong to God, who loves us without conditions, we can live as he does. The great conversion called for by Jesus is to move from belonging to the world to belonging to God.

The Return of the Prodigal Son

The "Ifs" That Enslave Me

As long as I keep running about asking "Do you love me? Do you really love me?" I give all power to the voices of the world and put myself in bondage because the world is filled with "ifs." The world says: "Yes, I love you *if* you are good-looking, intelligent, and wealthy. I love you *if* you have a good education, a good job, and good connections. I love you *if* you produce much, sell much, and buy much." There are endless "ifs" hidden in the world's love. These "ifs" enslave me, since it is impossible to respond adequately to all of them. The world's love is and always will be conditional. As long as I keep looking for my true self in the world of conditional love, I will remain "hooked" to the world—trying, failing, and trying again. It is a world that fosters addictions because what it offers cannot satisfy the deepest craving of my heart.

The Return of the Prodigal Son

The Truth About Me

You have to keep unmasking the world about you for what it is: manipulative, controlling, power-hungry, and, in the long run, destructive. The world tells you many lies about who you are, and you simply have to be realistic enough to remind yourself of this. Every time you feel hurt, offended, or rejected, you have to dare to say to yourself: "These feelings, strong as they may be, are not telling me the truth about myself. The truth, even though I cannot feel it right now, is that I am the chosen child of God, precious in God's eyes, called the Beloved from all eternity, and held safe in an everlasting embrace."

Life of the Beloved

God Longs to Bring Me Home

For most of my life I have struggled to find God, to know God, to love God. I have tried hard to follow the guidelines of the spiritual life—pray always, work for others, read the Scriptures—and to avoid the many temptations to dissipate myself. I have failed many times but always tried again, even when I was close to despair.

Now I wonder whether I have sufficiently realized that during all this time God has been trying to find me, to know me, and to love me. The question is not "How am I to find God?" but "How am I to let myself be found by him?" The question is not "How am I to know God?" but "How am I to let myself be known by God?" And, finally, the question is not "How am I to love God?" but "How am I to let myself be loved by God?" God is looking into the distance for me, trying to find me, and longing to bring me home.

The Return of the Prodigal Son

Embracing the True Self

The secular or false self is the self that is fabricated, as Thomas Merton says, by social compulsions. "Compulsive" is indeed the best adjective for the false self. It points to the need for ongoing and increasing affirmation. Who am I? I am the one who is liked, praised, admired, disliked, hated, or despised. . . . If being busy is a good thing, then I must be busy. If having money is a sign of real freedom, then I must claim my money. If knowing many people proves my importance, I will have to make the necessary contacts. The compulsion manifests itself in the lurking fear of failing and the steady urge to prevent this by gathering more of the same—more work, more money, more friends.

These very compulsions are at the basis of the two main enemies of the spiritual life: anger and greed. They are the inner side of the secular life, the sour fruits of our worldly dependences.

The Way of the Heart

Freedom Is Our Goal

While fear and anger are the most natural and most obvious reactions to a state of emergency, they have to be unmasked as expressions of our false selves. When we are trembling with fear or seething with anger, we have sold ourselves to the world or to a false god. Fear and anger take our freedom away and make us victims of the strong seductions of our world. Fear, as well as anger, when we look at them in solitude and quiet, reveal to us how deeply our sense of worth is dependent either on our success in the world or on the opinions of others. We suddenly realize that we have become what we do or what others think of us.

Clowning in Rome

Accept Your Whole Self—the Light and the Dark

I t is very difficult for each of us to believe in Christ's words, "I did not come to call the virtuous, but sinners. . . ." Perhaps no psychologist has stressed the need of self-acceptance as the way to self-realization so much as Carl Jung. For Jung, self-realization meant the integration of the shadow. It is the growing ability to allow the dark side of our personality to enter into our awareness and thus prevent a one-sided life in which only that which is presentable to the outside world is considered as a real part of ourselves. To come to an inner unity, totality and wholeness, every part of our self should be accepted and integrated. Christ represents the light in us. But Christ was crucified between two murderers and we cannot deny them, and certainly not the murderers who live in us.

Intimacy

January

18

Let God Be the Master of Your House

t strikes me increasingly just how hard-pressed people are nowadays. It's as though they're tearing about from one emergency to another. Never solitary, never still, never really free but always busy about something that just can't wait. You get the impression that, amid this frantic hurly-burly, we lose touch with life itself. We have the experience of being busy while nothing real seems to happen. The more agitated we are, and the more compacted our lives become, the more difficult it is to keep a space where God can let something truly new really take place.

The discipline of the heart helps us to let God into our hearts so that God can become known to us there, in the deepest recesses of our own being.

Letters to Marc About Jesus

You Are at Home While Still on the Way

When God has become our shepherd, our refuge, our fortress, then we can reach out to him in the midst of a broken world and feel at home while still on the way. When God dwells in us, we can enter into a wordless dialogue with him while still waiting on the day that he will lead us into the house where he has prepared a place for us (John 14:2). Then we can wait while we have already arrived and ask while we have already received. Then, indeed, we can comfort each other with the words of Paul (Philippians 4:6–7):

> There is no need to worry; but if there is anything you need, pray for it, asking God for it with prayer and thanksgiving, and that peace of God, which is so much greater than we can understand, will guard your hearts and your thoughts, in Christ Jesus.

Reaching Out

Learn to Trust God

Most of us distrust God. Most of us think of God as a fearful, punitive authority or as an empty, powerless nothing. Jesus' core message was that God is neither a powerless weakling nor a powerful boss, but a lover, whose only desire is to give us what our hearts most desire.

To pray is to listen to that voice of love. That is what obedience is all about. The word *obedience* comes from the Latin word *ob-audire,* which means "to listen with great attentiveness." Without listening, we become "deaf" to the voice of love. The Latin word for deaf is *surdus.* To be completely deaf is to be *absurdus,* yes, absurd. When we no longer pray, no longer listen to the voice of love that speaks to us in the moment, our lives become absurd lives in which we are thrown back and forth between the past and the future.

If we could just be, for a few minutes each day, fully where we are, we would indeed discover that we are not alone and that the One who is with us wants only one thing: to give us love.

Here and Now

God's Love Blows Where It Pleases

God cannot be understood: he cannot be grasped by the human mind. The truth escapes our human capacities. The only way to come close to it is by a constant emphasis on the limitations of our human capacities to "have" or "hold" the truth. We can neither explain God nor his presence in history. As soon as we identify God with any specific event or situation, we play God and distort the truth. We only can be faithful in our affirmation that God has not deserted us but calls us in the middle of all the unexplainable absurdities of life. It is very important to be deeply aware of this. There is a great and subtle temptation to suggest to myself or to others where God is working or where not, when he is present and when not; but nobody, no Christian, no priest, no monk, has any "special" knowledge about God. God cannot be limited by any human concept or prediction. He is greater than our mind and heart and perfectly free to reveal himself where and when he wants.

The Genesee Diary

Your Life Is Guided by God

To walk in the presence of the Lord means to move forward in life in such a way that all our desires, thoughts, and actions are constantly guided by him. When we walk in the Lord's presence, everything we see, hear, touch, or taste reminds us of him. This is what is meant by a prayerful life. It is not a life in which we say many prayers, but a life in which nothing, absolutely nothing, is done, said, or understood independently of him who is the origin and purpose of our existence. This is powerfully expressed by the nineteenth-century Russian Orthodox starets Theophan the Recluse:

> Into every duty a God-fearing heart must be put, a heart constantly permeated by the thought of God; and this will be the door through which the soul will enter into active life. . . . The essence is to be established in the remembrance of God, and to walk in his presence.[*]

The Living Reminder

---

[*] Theophan the Recluse, as quoted in Igumen Charitron, *The Art of Prayer,* ed. Timothy Ware (London: Faber and Faber, 1966), pp. 85, 98.

Be in the World Without Being of the World

B eing in the world without being of the world." These words summarize well the way Jesus speaks of the spiritual life. It is a life in which we are totally transformed by the Spirit of Love. Yet it is a life in which everything seems to remain the same. To live a spiritual life does not mean that we must leave our families, give up our jobs, or change our ways of working; it does not mean that we have to withdraw from social or political activities, or lose interest in literature and art; it does not require severe forms of asceticism or long hours of prayer. Changes such as these may in fact grow out of our spiritual life, and for some people radical decisions may be necessary. But the spiritual life can be lived in as many ways as there are people. What is new is that we have moved from the many things to the Kingdom of God. What is new is that we are set free from the compulsions of our world and have set our hearts on the only necessary thing. What is new is that we no longer experience the many things, people, and events as endless causes for worry, but begin to experience them as the rich variety of ways in which God makes his presence known to us.

Making All Things New

The House of Love

D o not be afraid, have no fear," is the voice we most need to hear. This voice was heard by Zechariah when Gabriel, the angel of the Lord, appeared to him in the temple and told him that his wife, Elizabeth, would bear a son; this voice was heard by Mary when the same angel entered her house in Nazareth and announced that she would conceive, bear a child, and name him Jesus; this voice was also heard by the women who came to the tomb and saw that the stone was rolled away. "Do not be afraid, do not be afraid, do not be afraid." The voice uttering these words sounds all through history as the voice of God's messengers, be they angels or saints. It is the voice that announces a whole new way of being, a being in the house of love, the house of the Lord. . . . The house of love is not simply a place in the afterlife, a place in heaven beyond this world. Jesus offers us this house right in the midst of our anxious world.

Lifesigns

All Is Clothed in Divine Light

God exists, and the meaning of all that I am depends totally on that knowledge. I wonder constantly if I am genuinely allowing my life to be determined by that truth. Maybe part of my reason for hesitating to embrace this truth fully is that it challenges me to give up all control over my life and to let God be God, my God, the God of my neighbor, and the God of all creation. But I also realize that as long as I do not "do" this, my life is an illusion and most of my energy is spoiled in trying to keep that illusion going.

Does all this mean that my thoughts, plans, projects, and ideas no longer matter? That conclusion has been drawn by people who used the spiritual life as a way to manipulate others, and that conclusion has led, sadly enough, to false views on asceticism, obedience, surrender to God's will, and certain forms of self-denial. The converted person does not say that nothing matters anymore, but that everything that is happens in God and that he is the dwelling place where we come to know the true order of things. Instead of saying: "Nothing matters anymore, since I know that God exists," the converted person says: "All is now clothed in divine light and, therefore, nothing can be unimportant."

Gracias!

Are You Home?

Today worrying means to be occupied and preoccupied with many things, while at the same time being bored, resentful, depressed, and very lonely. I am not trying to say that all of us are worried in such an extreme way all the time. Yet there is little doubt in my mind that the experience of being filled yet unfulfilled touches most of us to some degree at some time. In our highly technological and competitive world, it is hard to avoid completely the forces that fill up our inner and outer space and disconnect us from our innermost selves, our fellow human beings, and our God.

One of the most notable characteristics of worrying is that it fragments our lives. The many things to do, to think about, to plan for, the many people to remember to visit, or to talk with, the many causes to attack or defend, all these pull us apart and make us lose our center. Worrying causes us to be "all over the place," but seldom at home. One way to express the spiritual crisis of our time is to say that most of us have an address but cannot be found there.

Making All Things New

Shift Your Point of Gravity

Jesus' response to our worry-filled lives is quite different. He asks us to shift the point of gravity, to relocate the center of our attention, to change our priorities. Jesus wants us to move from the "many things" to the "one necessary thing." It is important for us to realize that Jesus in no way wants us to leave our many-faceted world. Rather, he wants us to live in it, but firmly rooted in the center of all things. Jesus does not speak about a change of activities, a change of contacts, or even a change of pace. He speaks about a change of heart. This change of heart makes everything different, even while everything appears to remain the same. This is the meaning of "Set your hearts on his kingdom first . . . and all these other things will be given you as well." What counts is where our hearts are. When we worry, we have our hearts in the wrong place. Jesus asks us to move our hearts to the center, where all other things fall into place.

Making All Things New

Become the Beloved

A s long as "being the Beloved" is little more than a beautiful thought or a lofty idea that hangs above my life to keep
me from becoming depressed, nothing really changes. What is
required is to become the Beloved in the commonplaces of my
daily existence, and bit by bit to close the gap that exists between
what I know myself to be and the countless realities of everyday
life. Becoming the Beloved is pulling the truth revealed to me
from above down into the ordinariness of what I am thinking
of, talking about, and doing from hour to hour.

Life of the Beloved

Taste the Moment to the Full

B e sure to taste the moment to the full. The Lord always reveals himself to you where you are most fully present. In
your prayer, try to present your anxieties, struggles, and fears to
him, and let him show you the way to follow him. More important than anything else is to follow the Lord. The rest is secondary. If you follow him, you can follow him as a priest, as a lay
minister, as a single person, or as a married person; but what
really counts is that he is the center.

Unpublished letter

A Prayer

Dear God,

I so much want to be in control.
I want to be the master of my own destiny.
Still I know that you are saying:
"Let me take you by the hand and lead you.
Accept my love
and trust that where I will bring you,
the deepest desires of your heart will be fulfilled."
Lord, open my hands to receive your gift of love.

Amen.

With Open Hands

FEBRUARY

My True Identity

The first thing that struck me when I came to live in a house with mentally handicapped people was that their liking and disliking me had absolutely nothing to do with the many useful things I had done until then. Since nobody could read my books, the books could not impress anyone, and since most of them never went to school, my twenty years at Notre Dame, Yale, and Harvard did not provide a significant introduction. . . . Not being able to use any of the skills that had proved so practical in the past was a real source of anxiety. I was suddenly faced with my naked self, open for affirmations and rejections, hugs and punches, smiles and tears, all dependent simply on how I was perceived at the moment. In a way, it seemed as though I was starting my life all over again. Relationships, connections, reputations could no longer be counted on.

The experience was and, in many ways, is still the most important experience of my new life, because it forced me to rediscover my true identity. These broken, wounded, and completely unpretentious people forced me to let go of my relevant self—the self that can do things, show things, prove things, build things—and forced me to reclaim that unadorned self in which I am completely vulnerable, open to receive and give love regardless of any accomplishments.

In the Name of Jesus

2
—

God Pitched His Tent Among Us

When St. John says that fear is driven out by perfect love, he points to a love that comes from God, a divine love. He does not speak about human affection, psychological compatibility, mutual attraction, or deep interpersonal feelings. All of that has its value and beauty, but the perfect love about which St. John speaks embraces and transcends all feelings, emotions, and passions. The perfect love that drives out all fear is the divine love in which we are invited to participate. The home, the intimate place, the place of true belonging, is, therefore, not a place made by human hands. It is fashioned for us by God, who came to pitch his tent among us, invite us to his place, and prepare a room for us in his own house.

Lifesigns

Love Deeply

D o not hesitate to love and to love deeply. You might be afraid of the pain that deep love can cause. When those you love deeply reject you, leave you, or die, your heart will be broken. But that should not hold you back from loving deeply. The pain that comes from deep love makes your love even more fruitful. It is like a plow that breaks the ground to allow the seed to take root and grow into a strong plant. Every time you experience the pain of rejection, absence, or death, you are faced with a choice. You can become bitter and decide not to love again, or you can stand straight in your pain and let the soil on which you stand become richer and more able to give life to new seeds.

The Inner Voice of Love

Love Bears Fruit

Against my own best intentions, I find myself continually striving to acquire power. When I give advice, I want to know whether it is being followed; when I offer help, I want to be thanked; when I give money, I want it to be used my way; when I do something good, I want to be remembered. I might not get a statue, or even a memorial plaque, but I am constantly concerned that I not be forgotten, that somehow I will live on in the thoughts and deeds of others.

But the father of the prodigal son is not concerned about himself. His long-suffering life has emptied him of his desires to keep in control of things. His children are his only concern; to them he wants to give himself completely, and for them he wants to pour out all of himself.

Can I give without wanting anything in return, love without putting any conditions on my love? Considering my immense need for human recognition and affection, I realize that it will be a lifelong struggle. But I am also convinced that each time I step over this need and act free of my concern for return, I can trust that my life can truly bear the fruits of God's Spirit.

The Return of the Prodigal Son

Joy of Life Comes from Living Well with Others

I n my own community, with many severely handicapped men and women, the greatest source of suffering is not the handicap itself, but the accompanying feelings of being useless, worthless, unappreciated, and unloved. It is much easier to accept the inability to speak, walk, or feed oneself than it is to accept the inability to be of special value to another person. We human beings can suffer immense deprivations with great steadfastness, but when we sense that we no longer have anything to offer to anyone, we quickly lose our grip on life. Instinctively we know that the joy of life comes from the ways in which we live together and that the pain of life comes from the many ways we fail to do that well.

Life of the Beloved

6

Loneliness

It is the most basic human loneliness that threatens us and is so hard to face. Too often we will do everything possible to avoid the confrontation with the experience of being alone, and sometimes we are able to create the most ingenious devices to prevent ourselves from being reminded of this condition. Our culture has become most sophisticated in the avoidance of pain, not only our physical pain but our emotional and mental pain as well. We not only bury our dead as if they were still alive, but we also bury our pains as if they were not really there. We have become so used to this state of anesthesia that we panic when there is nothing or nobody left to distract us. When we have no project to finish, no friend to visit, no book to read, no television to watch, or no record to play, and when we are left all alone by ourselves, we are brought so close to the revelation of our basic human aloneness and are so afraid of experiencing an all-pervasive sense of loneliness that we will do anything to get busy again and continue the game that makes us believe that everything is fine after all.

Reaching Out

Find the Source of Your Loneliness

Whenever you feel lonely, you must try to find the source of this feeling. You are inclined either to run away from your loneliness or to dwell in it. When you run away from it, your loneliness does not really diminish; you simply force it out of your mind temporarily. When you start dwelling in it, your feelings only become stronger, and you slip into depression.

The spiritual task is not to escape your loneliness, not to let yourself drown in it, but to find its source. This is not so easy to do, but when you can somehow identify the place from which these feelings emerge, they will lose some of their power over you. This identification is not an intellectual task; it is a task of the heart. With your heart you must search for that place without fear.

This is an important search because it leads you to discern something good about yourself. The pain of your loneliness may be rooted in your deepest vocation. You might find that your loneliness is linked to your call to live completely for God. Thus your loneliness may be revealed to you as the other side of your unique gift. Once you can experience in your innermost being the truth of this, you may find your loneliness not only tolerable but even fruitful. What seemed primarily painful may then become a feeling that, though painful, opens for you the way to an even deeper knowledge of God's love.

The Inner Voice of Love

From Loneliness to Solitude

To live a spiritual life we must first find the courage to enter into the desert of our loneliness and to change it by gentle and persistent efforts into a garden of solitude. This requires not only courage but also a strong faith. As hard as it is to believe that the dry desolate desert can yield endless varieties of flowers, it is equally hard to imagine that our loneliness is hiding unknown beauty. The movement from loneliness to solitude, however, is the beginning of any spiritual life because it is a movement from the restless senses to the restful spirit, from the outward-reaching cravings to the inward-reaching search, from the fearful clinging to the fearless play.

Reaching Out

Loneliness Is an Invitation

The Christian way of life does not take away our loneliness; it protects and cherishes it as a precious gift.

Sometimes it seems as if we do everything possible to avoid the painful confrontation with our basic human loneliness, and allow ourselves to be trapped by false gods promising immediate satisfaction and quick relief. But perhaps the painful awareness of loneliness is an invitation to transcend our limitations and look beyond the boundaries of our existence. The awareness of loneliness might be a gift we must protect and guard, because our loneliness reveals to us an inner emptiness that can be destructive when misunderstood, but filled with promise for those who can tolerate its sweet pain.

The Wounded Healer

Solitude Makes Real Fellowship Possible

By slowly converting our loneliness into a deep solitude, we create that precious space where we can discover the voice telling us about our inner necessity—that is, our vocation. Unless our questions, problems, and concerns are tested and matured in solitude, it is not realistic to expect answers that are really our own.... This is a very difficult task, because in our world we are constantly pulled away from our innermost self and encouraged to look for answers instead of listening to the questions. A lonely person has no inner time or inner rest to wait and listen. He wants answers and wants them here and now. But in solitude we can pay attention to the inner self. This has nothing to do with egocentrism or unhealthy introspection because in the words of [Rainer Maria] Rilke, "what is going on in your innermost being is worthy of your whole love."* In solitude we can become present to ourselves.... There we also can become present to others by reaching out to them, not greedy for attention and affection but offering our own selves to help build a community of love. Solitude does not pull us away from our fellow human beings but instead makes real fellowship possible.

Reaching Out

---

* Rainer Maria Rilke, *Letters to a Young Poet* (New York: Norton, 1954), pp. 18–19.

A New Way to Be Human

The love of God is an unconditional love, and only that love can empower us to live together without violence. When we know that God loves us deeply and will always go on loving us, whoever we are and whatever we do, it becomes possible to expect no more of our fellow men and women than they are able to give, to forgive them generously when they have offended us, and always to respond to their hostility with love. By doing so we make visible a new way of being human and a new way of responding to our world problems.

Letters to Marc About Jesus

Claim Your Truth

I t seems crucial that you realize deeply that your worth and value does not depend on anyone else. You have to claim your own inner truth. You are a person worth being loved and called to give love, not because anyone says so . . . but because you are created out of love and live in the embrace of a God who didn't hesitate to send his only son to die for us. . . . Your being good and worthy of love does not depend on any human being. You have to keep saying to yourself: "I am being loved by an unconditional, unlimited love and that love allows me to be a free person, center of my own actions and decisions." The more you can come to realize this, the more you will be able to forgive those who have hurt you and love them in their brokenness. Without a deep feeling of self-respect, you cannot forgive and will always feel anger, resentment, and revenge. The greatest human act is forgiveness: "Forgive us our sins, as we forgive those who have sinned against us." Forgiveness stands in the center of God's love for us and also in the center of our love for each other. Loving one another means forgiving one another over and over again.

Love, Henri

Make God's Unconditional Love Visible

Whenever, contrary to the world's vindictiveness, we love our enemy, we exhibit something of the perfect love of God, whose will is to bring all human beings together as children of one Father. Whenever we forgive instead of getting angry at one another, bless instead of cursing one another, tend one another's wounds instead of rubbing salt into them, hearten instead of discouraging one another, give hope instead of driving one another to despair, hug instead of harassing one another, welcome instead of cold-shouldering one another, thank instead of criticizing one another, praise instead of maligning one another . . . in short, whenever we opt for and not against one another, we make God's unconditional love visible; we are diminishing violence and giving birth to a new community.

Letters to Marc About Jesus

Lead a Loving Life

S elf-knowledge and self-love are the fruit of knowing and
loving God. You can see better then what is intended by
the great commandment to "love the Lord your God with all
your heart, with all your soul, and with all your mind, and to
love your neighbor as yourself." Laying our hearts totally open
to God leads to a love of ourselves that enables us to give whole-
hearted love to our fellow human beings. In the seclusion of our
hearts we learn to know the hidden presence of God; and with
that spiritual knowledge we can lead a loving life.

Letters to Marc About Jesus

Enter the House of Love

When we enter into the household of God, we come to realize that the fragmentation of humanity and its agony grow from the false supposition that all human beings have to fight for their right to be appreciated and loved. In the house of God's love we come to see with new eyes and hear with new ears and thus recognize all people, whatever their race, religion, sex, wealth, intelligence, or background, belong to that same house. God's house has no dividing walls or closed doors. "I am the door," Jesus says. "Anyone who enters through me will be safe" (John 10:9). The more fully we enter into the house of love, the more clearly we see that we are there together with all humanity and that in and through Christ we are brothers and sisters, members of one family.

Lifesigns

The True Voice of Love

Fear is the great enemy of intimacy. Fear makes us run away from each other or cling to each other, but does not create true intimacy. When Jesus was arrested in the Garden of Gethsemane, the disciples were overcome by fear and they all "deserted him and ran away" (Matthew 26:56). . . . Fear makes us move away from each other to a "safe" distance, or move toward each other to a "safe" closeness, but fear does not create the space where true intimacy can exist. . . .

To those who are tortured by inner or outer fear, and who desperately look for the house of love where they can find the intimacy their hearts desire, Jesus says: "You have a home . . . I am your home . . . claim me as your home . . . you will find it to be the intimate place where I have found my home . . . it is right where you are . . . in your innermost being . . . in your heart." The more attentive we are to such words the more we realize that we do not have to go far to find what we are searching for. The tragedy is that we are so possessed by fear that we do not trust our innermost self as an intimate place but anxiously wander around hoping to find it where we are not. We try to find that intimate place in knowledge, competence, notoriety, success, friends, sensations, pleasure, dreams, or artificially induced states of consciousness. Thus we become strangers to ourselves, people who have an address but are never home and hence cannot be addressed by the true voice of love.

Lifesigns

Create Space for the Stranger

I n our world full of strangers, estranged from their own past, culture, and country, from their neighbors, friends, and family, from their deepest self and their God, we witness a painful search for a hospitable place where life can be lived without fear and where community can be found. Although many, we might say even most, strangers in this world become easily the victim of a fearful hostility, it is possible for men and women and obligatory for Christians to offer an open and hospitable space where strangers can cast off their strangeness and become our fellow human beings. The movement from hostility to hospitality is hard and full of difficulties. Our society seems to be increasingly full of fearful, defensive, aggressive people, anxiously clinging to their property and inclined to look at their surrounding world with suspicion, always expecting an enemy to suddenly appear, intrude, and do harm. But still—that is our vocation: to convert the *hostis* into a *hospes*, the enemy into a guest, and to create the free and fearless space where brotherhood and sisterhood can be formed and fully experienced.

Reaching Out

Hospitality

Hospitality means primarily the creation of a free space where the stranger can enter and become a friend instead of an enemy. Hospitality is not to change people but to offer them space where change can take place. It is not to bring men and women over to our side, but to offer freedom not disturbed by dividing lines. . . . The paradox of hospitality is that it wants to create emptiness, not a fearful emptiness, but a friendly emptiness where strangers can enter and discover themselves as created free; free to sing their own songs, speak their own languages, dance their own dances; free also to leave and follow their own vocations. Hospitality is not a subtle invitation to adore the lifestyle of the host, but the gift of a chance for the guest to find his own.

Reaching Out

Being at Home

Creating space for the other is far from an easy task. It requires hard concentration and articulate work. . . . Indeed, more often than not, rivalry and competition, desire for power and immediate results, impatience and frustration, and most of all, plain fear make their forceful demands and tend to fill every possible empty corner of our life. Empty space tends to create fear. As long as our minds, hearts, and hands are occupied, we can avoid confronting the painful questions to which we never gave much attention and that we do not want to surface. . . .

When we think back to the places where we felt most at home, we quickly see that it was where our hosts gave us the precious freedom to come and go on our own terms and did not claim us for their own needs. Only in a free space can re-creation take place and new life be found. The real host is the one who offers that space where we do not have to be afraid and where we can listen to our own inner voices and find our own personal way of being human. But to be such a host we have to first of all be at home in our own house.

Reaching Out

Human Intimacy

A mature human intimacy requires a deep and profound respect for the free and empty space that needs to exist within and between partners and that asks for a continuous mutual protection and nurture. Only in this way can a relationship be lasting, precisely because mutual love is experienced as a participation in a greater and earlier love to which it points. In this way intimacy can be rich and fruitful, since it has been given carefully protected space in which to grow. This relationship no longer is a fearful clinging to each other but a free dance, allowing space in which we can move forward and backward, form constantly new patterns, and see each other as always new.

Clowning in Rome

The Table Is the Place of Intimacy

The table is the place of intimacy. Around the table we discover each other. It's the place where we pray. It's the place where we ask: "How was your day?" It's the place where we eat and drink together and say: "Come on, take some more!" It is the place of old and new stories. It is the place of smiles and tears. The table, too, is the place where distance is most painfully felt. It is the place where the children feel the tension between the parents, where brothers and sisters express their anger and jealousies, where accusations are made, and where plates and cups become instruments of violence. Around the table, we know whether there is friendship and community or hatred and division. Precisely because the table is the place of intimacy for all the members of the household, it is also the place where the absence of that intimacy is most painfully revealed.

With Burning Hearts

Human Intimacy Creates a Home for God

M arriage is not a lifelong attraction of two individuals to each other, but a call for two people to witness together to God's love. . . . [The] intimacy of marriage itself is an intimacy that is based on the common participation in a love greater than the love two people can offer each other. The real mystery of marriage is not that [two people] love each other so much that they can find God in each other's lives, but that God loves them so much that they can discover each other more and more as living reminders of God's divine presence. They are brought together, indeed, as two prayerful hands extended toward God and forming in this way a home for God in this world.

The same is true for friendship. Deep and mature friendship does not mean that we keep looking each other in the eyes and are constantly impressed or enraptured by each other's beauty, talents, and gifts, but it means that together we look at God, who calls us to God's service.

Clowning in Rome

Birthdays

Birthdays need to be celebrated. I think it is more important to celebrate a birthday than a successful exam, a promotion, or a victory. Because to celebrate a birthday means to say to someone: "Thank you for being you." Celebrating a birthday is exalting life and being glad for it. On a birthday we do not say: "Thanks for what you did, or said, or accomplished." No, we say: "Thank you for being born and being among us."

On birthdays we celebrate the present. We do not complain about what happened or speculate about what will happen, but we lift someone up and let everyone say: "We love you."

Here and Now

24

Children Are Our Guests

I t belongs to the center of the Christian message that children are not properties to own and rule over, but gifts to cherish and care for. Our children are our most important guests, who enter into our home, ask for careful attention, stay for a while, and then leave to follow their own way. Children are strangers whom we have to get to know.

Reaching Out

Protect Your Inner Sanctuary

There is a false form of honesty that suggests that nothing should remain hidden and that everything should be said, expressed, and communicated. This honesty can be very harmful, and if it does not harm, it at least makes the relationship flat, superficial, empty, and often very boring. When we try to shake off our loneliness by creating a milieu without limiting boundaries, we may become entangled in a stagnating closeness. It is our vocation to prevent the harmful exposure of our inner sanctuary, not only for our own protection but also as a service to our fellow human beings with whom we want to enter in a creative communion. Just as words lose their power when they are not born out of silence, so openness loses its meaning when there is no ability to be closed.

Reaching Out

Burnout

Aren't you, like me, hoping that some person, thing, or event will come along to give you that final feeling of inner well-being you desire? Don't you often hope: "May this book, idea, course, trip, job, country, or relationship fulfill my deepest desire"? But as long as you are waiting for that mysterious moment you will go on running helter-skelter, always anxious and restless, always lustful and angry, never fully satisfied. You know that this is the compulsiveness that keeps us going and busy but at the same time makes us wonder whether we are getting anywhere in the long run. This is the way to spiritual exhaustion and burnout.

Life of the Beloved

God's Kingdom Is Within

The words of Jesus "Set your hearts on God's kingdom first . . . and all other things will be given you as well" summarize best the way we are called to live our lives. With our hearts set on God's kingdom. That kingdom is not some faraway land that we hope to reach, nor is it life after death or an ideal state of affairs. No. God's Kingdom is, first of all, the active presence of God's Spirit within us, offering us the freedom we truly desire.

And so the main question becomes: how do we set our hearts on the Kingdom first when our hearts are preoccupied with so many things? Somehow a radical change of heart is required, a change that allows us to experience the reality of our existence from God's place.

Here and Now

You Belong to God

You are not what you do, although you do a lot. You are not what you have collected in terms of friendships and connections, although you might have many. You are not the popularity that you have received. You are not the success of your work. You are not what people say about you, whether they speak well or whether they speak poorly about you. All these things that keep you quite busy, quite occupied, and often quite preoccupied are not telling the truth about who you are. I am here to remind you in the name of God that you are the Beloved Daughters and Sons of God, and that God says to you, "I have called you from all eternity and you are engraved from all eternity in the palms of my hands. You are mine. You belong to me, and I love you with an everlasting love."

"Belovedness"

A Prayer

Dear Lord,

I bring before you all the people who experience failure in their search for a creative, affectionate relationship. Many single people feel lonely and unable to sustain a friendship for a long period of time; many married people feel frustrated in their marriage and separate to go different ways; many children cannot speak to their parents; and many parents have become afraid of their children. All around me I see the hunger for love and the inability to experience it in a deep and lasting way.

O Lord, look with favor on us, your people, and impart your love to us—not as an idea or concept, but as a lived experience. We can only love each other because you have loved us first. Let us know that first love so that we can see all human love as a reflection of a greater love, a love without conditions and limitations.

Heal those who feel hurt in their most intimate self, who feel rejected, misunderstood, or even misused. Show them your healing love, and help them on the way to forgiveness and reconciliation.

Amen.

A Cry for Mercy

MARCH

Jesus at the Center

I f you were to ask me point-blank: "What does it mean to you to live spiritually?" I would have to reply: "Living with Jesus at the center." . . . When I look back over the last thirty years of my life, I can say that, for me, the person of Jesus has come to be more and more important. Specifically, this means that what matters increasingly is getting to know Jesus and living in solidarity with him.

Letters to Marc About Jesus

Listen to God

Everything we know about Jesus indicates that he was concerned with only one thing: to do the will of his Father. Nothing in the Gospels is as impressive as Jesus' single-minded obedience to his Father. From his first recorded words in the Temple, "Did you not know that I must be busy with my Father's affairs?" (Luke 2:49), to his last words on the cross, "Father, into your hands I commend my spirit" (Luke 23:46), Jesus' only concern was to do the will of his Father. He says, "The Son can do nothing by himself; he can do only what he sees the Father doing" (John 5:19). . . .

Jesus is the obedient one. The center of his life is this obedient relationship with the Father. This may be hard for us to understand because the word *obedience* has so many negative connotations in our society. It makes us think of authority figures who impose their wills against our desires. It makes us remember unhappy childhood events or hard tasks performed under threats of punishment. But none of this applies to Jesus' obedience. His obedience means a total, fearless listening to his loving Father. Between the Father and the Son there is only love.

Making All Things New

A Converted Life

Living a spiritual life requires a change of heart, a conversion. Such a conversion may be marked by a sudden inner change, or it can take place through a long, quiet process of transformation. But it always involves an inner experience of oneness. We realize that we are in the center, and that from there all that is and all that takes place can be seen and understood as part of the mystery of God's life with us. Our conflicts and pains, our tasks and promises, our families and friends, our activities and projects, our hopes and aspirations, no longer appear to us a fatiguing variety of things that we can barely keep together, but rather as affirmations and revelations of the new life of the Spirit in us. "All these other things," which so occupied and preoccupied us, now come as gifts or challenges that strengthen and deepen the new life that we have discovered. This does not mean that the spiritual life makes things easier or takes our struggles and pains away. The lives of Jesus' disciples clearly show that suffering does not diminish because of conversion. Sometimes it even becomes more intense. But our attention is no longer directed to the "more or less." What matters is to listen attentively to the Spirit and to go obediently where we are being led, whether to a joyful or a painful place.

Poverty, pain, struggle, anguish, agony, and even inner darkness may continue to be part of our experience. They may even be God's way of purifying us. But life is no longer boring, resentful, depressing, or lonely because we have come to know that everything that happens is part of our way to the Father.

Making All Things New

Jesus Is God-Who-Suffers-with-Us

God sent Jesus to make free persons of us. He has chosen compassion as the way to freedom. That is a great deal more radical than you might at first imagine. It means that God wanted to liberate us, not by removing suffering from us, but by sharing it with us. Jesus is God-who-suffers-with-us. Over time, the word *sympathizing* has become a somewhat feeble way of expressing the reality of "suffering with" someone. Nowadays, when someone says: "I have sympathy for you," it has a rather distant ring about it. The feeling, at least for me, is of someone looking down from above. The word's original meaning of "suffering together with someone" has been partly lost. That's why I've opted for the word *compassion*. It's warmer, more intimate, and closer. It's taking part in the suffering of the other, being totally a fellow human being in suffering. . . .

Jesus is the revelation of God's unending, unconditional love for us human beings. Everything that Jesus has done, said, and undergone is meant to show us that the love we most long for is given to us by God, not because we deserved it, but because God is a God of love.

Letters to Marc About Jesus

Pruning

Jesus said, "I am the true vine, and my Father is the vine-dresser. Every branch in me that bears no fruit he cuts away, and every branch that does bear fruit he prunes, to make it bear even more" (John 15:1–2).

These words open a new perspective on suffering for me. Pruning helps trees to bear more fruit. Even when I bear fruit, even when I do things for God's kingdom, even when people express gratitude for coming to know Jesus through me, I need a lot more pruning. Many unnecessary branches and twigs prevent the vine from bearing all the fruit it can. They have to be clipped off. This is a painful process, all the more so because I do not know that they are unnecessary. They often seem beautiful, charming, and very alive. But they need to be cut away so that more fruit can grow.

It helps me to think about painful rejections, moments of loneliness, feelings of inner darkness and despair, and lack of support and human affection as God's pruning. I am aware that I might have settled too soon for the few fruits that I can recognize in my life. I might say, "Well, I am doing some good here and there, and I should be grateful for and content with the little good I do." But that might be false modesty and even a form of spiritual laziness. God calls me to more. God wants to prune me. A pruned vine does not look beautiful, but during harvest time it produces much fruit. The great challenge is to continue to recognize God's pruning hand in my life. Then I can avoid resentment and depression and become even more grateful that I am called upon to bear even more fruit than I thought I could. Suffering then becomes a way of purification and allows me to rejoice in its fruits with deep gratitude and without pride.

Take Up Your Cross

Your pain is deep, and it won't just go away. It is also uniquely yours, because it is linked to some of your earliest life experiences.

Your call is to bring that pain home. As long as your wounded part remains foreign to your adult self, your pain will injure you as well as others. Yes, you have to incorporate your pain into your self and let it bear fruit in your heart and the hearts of others.

This is what Jesus means when he asks you to take up your cross. He encourages you to recognize and embrace your unique suffering and to trust that your way to salvation lies therein. Taking up your cross means, first of all, befriending your wounds and letting them reveal to you your own truth.

There is great pain and suffering in the world. But the pain hardest to bear is your own. Once you have taken up that cross, you will be able to see clearly the crosses that others have to bear, and you will be able to reveal to them their own ways to joy, peace, and freedom.

The Inner Voice of Love

From Action to Surrender

I t is important for me to realize that Jesus fulfills his mission
not by what he does, but by what is done to him. Just as with
everyone else, most of my life is determined by what is done
to me and thus is passion. And because most of my life is passion, things being done to me, only small parts of my life are
determined by what I think, say, or do. I am inclined to protest
against this and to want all to be action originated by me. But
the truth is that my passion is a much greater part of my life
than my action. Not to recognize this is self-deception and not
to embrace my passion with love is self-rejection.

It is good news to know that Jesus is handed over to passion,
and through his passion accomplishes his divine task on earth.
It is good news for a world passionately searching for wholeness.

Jesus' words to Peter remind me that Jesus' transition from
action to passion must also be ours if we want to follow his way.
He says, "When you were young you put on your own belt and
walked where you liked; but when you grow old you will stretch
out your hands, and somebody else will put a belt round you
and take you where you would rather not go" (John 21:18).

The Road to Daybreak

Let Yourself Be Loved

I deeply know that I have a home in Jesus, just as Jesus has a home in God. I know, too, that when I abide in Jesus I abide with him in God. "Those who love me," Jesus says, "will be loved by my Father" (John 14:21). My true spiritual work is to let myself be loved, fully and completely, and to trust that in that love I will come to the fulfillment of my vocation. I keep trying to bring my wandering, restless, anxious self home, so that I can rest there in the embrace of love.

Sabbatical Journey

Waiting in Expectation

Jesus said to his disciples, "A little while, and you will no longer see me, and again a little while, and you will see me" (John 16:16).

Life is "a little while," a short moment of waiting. But life is not empty waiting. It is to wait full of expectation. The knowledge that God will indeed fulfill the promise to renew everything, and will offer us a "new heaven and a new earth," makes the waiting exciting. We can already see the beginning of the fulfillment. Nature speaks of it every spring; people [speak] of it whenever they smile; the sun, the moon, and the stars speak of it when [they] offer us light and beauty; and all of history speaks of it when amid all devastation and chaos, men and women arise who reveal the hope that lives within them. . . . What is my main task during my "little while"? I want to point to the signs of the Kingdom to come, to speak about the first rays of the day of God, to witness to the many manifestations of the Holy Spirit among us. I do not want to complain about this passing world but to focus on the eternal that lights up in the midst of the temporal. I yearn to create space where it can be seen and celebrated.

Sabbatical Journey

A Spirituality of Waiting

Increasingly in our society we feel we have less and less influence on the decisions that affect our own existence. Therefore it becomes increasingly important to recognize that the largest part of our existence involves waiting in the sense of being acted upon. The life of Jesus tells us that not being in control is part of the human condition. His vocation and ours are fulfilled not just in action but also in passion, waiting.

Imagine how important this message is for us and for the people in our world. If it is true that God in Jesus Christ is waiting for our response to divine love, then we can discover a whole new perspective on how to wait in life. We can learn to be obedient people who do not always try to go back to the action but recognize the fulfillment of our deepest humanity in passion, in waiting. If we can do this, I am convinced that we will come in touch with the power and the glory of God and our own new life. Our service to others will include our helping them see the glory breaking through—not only where they are active but also where they are being acted upon. And so the spirituality of waiting is not simply our waiting for God. It is also participating in God's own waiting for us and in that way coming to share in the deepest love, which is God's love.

Finding My Way Home

Patience

The mother of expectation is patience. The French author Simone Weil writes in her notebooks: "Waiting patiently in expectation is the foundation of the spiritual life." Without patience our expectation degenerates into wishful thinking. Patience comes from the word *patior,* which means "to suffer." The first thing that Jesus promises is suffering: "I tell you . . . you will be weeping and wailing . . . and you will be sorrowful." But he calls these birth pains. And so, what seems a hindrance becomes a way; what seems an obstacle becomes a door; what seems a misfit becomes a cornerstone. Jesus changes our history from a random series of sad incidents and accidents into a constant opportunity for a change of heart. To wait patiently, therefore, means to allow our weeping and wailing to become the purifying preparation by which we are made ready to receive the joy that is promised to us.

Out of Solitude

Your Hearts Will Be Full of Joy

Whereas patience is the mother of expectation, it is expectation itself that brings new joy to our lives. Jesus not only made us look at our pains, but also beyond them. "You are sad now, but I shall see you again and your hearts will be full of joy." A man or woman without hope in the future cannot live creatively in the present. The paradox of expectation indeed is that those who believe in tomorrow can better live today, that those who expect joy to come out of sadness can discover the beginnings of a new life in the center of the old, that those who look forward to the returning Lord can discover him already in their midst.

Out of Solitude

The Descending Way of Jesus

Jesus presents to us the great mystery of the descending way. It is the way of suffering, but also the way to healing. It is the way of humiliation, but also the way to the resurrection. It is the way of tears, but of tears that turn into tears of joy. It is the way of hiddenness, but also the way that leads to the light that will shine for all people. It is the way of persecution, oppression, martyrdom, and death, but also the way to the full disclosure of God's love. In the Gospel of John, Jesus says: "As Moses lifted up the snake in the desert, so must the Son of man be lifted up" (John 3:14–15). You see in these words how the descending way of Jesus becomes the ascending way. The "lifting up" that Jesus speaks of refers both to his being raised up on the cross in total humiliation and to his being raised up from the dead in total glorification. . . .

Each one of us has to seek out his or her own descending way of love. That calls for much prayer, much patience, and much guidance. It has nothing at all to do with spiritual heroics, dramatically throwing everything overboard to "follow" Jesus. The descending way is a way that is concealed in each person's heart. But because it is so seldom walked on, it's often overgrown with weeds. Slowly but surely we have to clear the weeds, open the way, and set out on it unafraid.

Letters to Marc About Jesus

Find Your Own Path to Love

Every time you make free time for God, you clear up a bit of the descending path, and you see where you can plant your feet on the way to love. Nothing spectacular or sensational. It may be simply a matter of what you say, what you read, to whom you speak, where you go on a free afternoon, or how you regard yourself and other people. What's fascinating is that the first step invariably makes the second one easier. You begin to discover that love begets love, and step-by-step you move further forward on the way to God. Gradually, you shed your misgivings about the way of love; you see that "in love there is no room for fear," and you feel yourself drawn to descend deeper and deeper on the way that Jesus walked before you.

Letters to Marc About Jesus

Everything That Belongs to Jesus Is Given for Us to Receive

Our lives are destined to become like the life of Jesus. The whole purpose of Jesus' ministry is to bring us to the house of his Father. Not only did Jesus come to free us from the bonds of sin and death; he also came to lead us into the intimacy of his divine life. It is difficult for us to imagine what this means. We tend to emphasize the distance between Jesus and ourselves. We see Jesus as the all-knowing and all-powerful Son of God who is unreachable for us sinful, broken human beings. But in thinking this way, we forget that Jesus came to give us his own life. He came to lift us up into loving community with the Father. Only when we recognize the radical purpose of Jesus' ministry will we be able to understand the meaning of the spiritual life. Everything that belongs to Jesus is given for us to receive. All that Jesus does we may also do.

Making All Things New

Does God Really Care?

The pressures of living in our society make us react to questions and problems more with bitterness, resentment, and even hatred. Far from being inspired, we seem to have forgotten about God. We are cynical about so much suffering in ourselves and in the world and we do not know how to integrate that with our spiritual aspirations. As in a love-hate relationship, feelings of deep disillusionment color our capacity to relate with the One we once accepted and tried to follow. We feel ambivalent and dissatisfied, wondering if God can really be trusted and if God really is a personal God who is "close to the brokenhearted."

We aren't questioning this with words, but our behavior betrays us. We say to a friend, "I will pray for you." But we walk away without any sense of a commitment to pray because we have doubts about prayers being answered. We listen to sermons and homilies affirming the benefits of a life of communion with God, but somewhere deep down we really believe that it is action, not prayer, that will satisfy our needs. We may think prayer is good when there is nothing more important to do, but we have strong reservations and doubts about God's effectiveness in our world, of God's personal interest in us. We are no longer conscious of *God-with-us*.

Clowning in Rome

Open Yourself to the Great Encounter

am not saying there is an easy solution to our ambivalent relationship with God. Solitude is not a solution. It is a direction. The direction is pointed to by the prophet Elijah, who did not find Yahweh in the mighty wind, the earthquake, the fire, but in the still, small voice; this direction, too, is indicated by Jesus, who chose solitude as the place to be with his Father. Every time we enter into solitude we withdraw from our windy, earthquaking, fiery lives and open ourselves to the great encounter. The first thing we often discover in solitude is our own restlessness, our drivenness, and compulsiveness, our urge to act quickly, to make an impact, and to have influence; and often we find it very hard to withstand the temptation to return as quickly as possible to the world of "relevance." But when we persevere with the help of a gentle discipline, we slowly come to hear the still, small voice and to feel the gentle breeze, and so come to know the Lord of our heart, soul, and mind, the Lord who makes us see who we really are.

Clowning in Rome

Dare to Stand in Your Suffering

I really want to encourage you not to despair, not to lose faith, not to let go of God in your life, but stand in your suffering as a person who believes that she is deeply loved by God. When you look inside yourself, you might sometimes be overwhelmed by all the brokenness and confusion, but when you look outside toward him who died on the cross for you, you might suddenly realize that your brokenness has been lived through for you long before you touched it yourself.

Suffering is a period in your life in which true faith can emerge, a naked faith, a faith that comes to life in the midst of great pain. The grain, indeed, has to die in order to bear fruit, and when you dare to stand in your suffering, your life will bear fruit in ways that are far beyond your own predications or understanding. . . . Spend some time each morning doing nothing but simply sitting in the presence of God and saying the Jesus Prayer.* Gradually, God will enter your heart in a new way and bring new light into your struggle.

Unpublished letter

---

* The Jesus Prayer Henri used: "Lord Jesus Christ, Son of the living God, have mercy on me a sinner."

God Forgives You

This morning I meditated on God's eagerness to forgive me, revealed in these words: "As far as the East is from the West, so far does God remove my sin" (Psalms 103:12). In the midst of all my distractions, I was touched by God's desire to forgive me again and again. If I return to God with a repentant heart after I have sinned, God is always there to embrace me and let me start afresh. "The Lord is full of compassion and love, slow to anger and rich in mercy."

It is hard for me to forgive someone who has really offended me, especially when it happens more than once. I begin to doubt the sincerity of the one who asks forgiveness for a second, third, or fourth time. But God does not keep count. God just waits for our return, without resentment or desire for revenge. God wants us home. "The love of the Lord is everlasting."

The Road to Daybreak

Live Under the Blessing

Jesus suffered and died for our sake. He suffered and died, not in despair, not as the rejected one, but as the Beloved Child of God. From the moment he heard the voice that said, "You are my Beloved, on you my favor rests," he lived his life and suffered his pain under the Blessing of the Father. He knew that even when everyone would run away from him, his Father would never leave him alone.

For us, the greatest temptation is to lose touch with the Blessing. We are Beloved Sons and Daughters of God. When we live our suffering under the Blessing, even the greatest pain, yes, even death, will lead us deeper into the forgiving and life-giving heart of God. But when we think we are not loved, when we reflect on ourselves as living under a curse, when we say or think: "I am not good," our suffering will lead us to despair and our death cannot give life.

Love, Henri

I Love You, I Love You, I Love You

The voice of despair says, "I sin over and over again. After endless promises to myself and others to do better next time, I find myself back again in the old dark places. Forget about trying to change. I have tried for years. It didn't work and it never will work. It is better that I get out of people's way, be forgotten, no longer around, dead."

This strangely attractive voice takes all uncertainties away and puts an end to the struggle. It speaks unambiguously for the darkness and offers a clear-cut negative identity.

But Jesus came to open my ears to another voice that says, "I am your God, I have molded you with my own hands, and I love what I have made. I love you with a love that has no limits, because I love you as I am loved. Do not run away from me. Come back to me—not once, not twice, but always again. You are my child. . . . I am your God—the God of mercy and compassion, the God of pardon and love, the God of tenderness and care. Please do not say that I have given up on you, that I cannot stand you anymore, that there is no way back. It is not true. I so much want you to be with me. I so much want you to be close to me. I know all your thoughts. I hear all your words. I see all your actions. And I love you because you are beautiful, made in my own image, an expression of my most intimate love. Do not judge yourself. Do not condemn yourself. Do not reject yourself. Let my love touch the deepest, most hidden corners of your heart and reveal to you your own beauty, a beauty that you have lost sight of, but that will become visible to you again in the light of my mercy. Come, come, let me wipe your tears, and let my mouth come close to your ear and say to you, 'I love you, I love you, I love you.'"

The Road to Daybreak

You Are a Spring of Eternal Life

In the midst of Lent I am made aware that Easter is coming again: the days are becoming longer, the snow is withdrawing, the sun is bringing new warmth, and a bird is singing. Yesterday, during the night prayers, a cat was crying! Indeed, spring announces itself. And tonight, O Lord, I heard you speak to the Samaritan woman. You said: "Anyone who drinks the water that I shall give you will never be thirsty again; the water that I shall give you will turn into a spring inside him, welling up to eternal life." What words! They are worth many hours, days, and weeks of reflection. I will carry them with me in my preparation for Easter. The water that you give turns into a spring. Therefore, I do not have to be stingy with your gift, O Lord. I can freely let the water spring from my center and let anyone who desires drink from it. Perhaps I will even see this spring myself when others come to it to quench their thirst.

A Cry for Mercy

Hope at All Times

I t is central in the biblical tradition that God's love for his people should not be forgotten. It should remain with us in the present. When everything is dark, when we are surrounded by despairing voices, when we do not see any exits, then we can find salvation in a remembered love, a love that is not simply a wistful recollection of a bygone past, but a living force that sustains us in the present. Through memory, love transcends the limits of time and offers hope at any moment of our lives.

The Living Reminder

Be Surprised by Joy

earn the discipline of being surprised not by suffering but by joy. As we grow old . . . there is suffering ahead of us, immense suffering, a suffering that will continue to tempt us to think that we have chosen the wrong road. . . . But don't be surprised by pain. Be surprised by joy, be surprised by the little flower that shows its beauty in the midst of a barren desert, and be surprised by the immense healing power that keeps bursting forth like springs of fresh water from the depth of our pain.

Finding My Way Home

God Is a God-with-Us

Again and again you see how Jesus opts for what is small, hidden, and poor, and accordingly declines to wield influence. His many miracles always serve to express his profound compassion with suffering humanity; never are they attempts to call attention to himself. As a rule, he even forbids those he has cured to talk to others about it. And as Jesus' life continues to unfold, he becomes increasingly aware that he has been called to fulfill his vocation in suffering and death. In all of this, it becomes plain to us that God has willed to show his love for the world by descending more and more deeply into human frailty.

Letters to Marc About Jesus

Jesus' Hiddenness

I don't think you'll ever be able to penetrate the mystery of God's revelation in Jesus until it strikes you that the major part of Jesus' life was hidden and that even the "public" years remained invisible as far as most people were concerned. Whereas the way of the world is to insist on publicity, celebrity, popularity, and getting maximum exposure, God prefers to work in secret. You must let that mystery of God's secrecy, God's anonymity, sink deeply into your consciousness because, otherwise, you're continually looking at it from the wrong point of view. In God's sight the things that really matter seldom take place in public. . . . Maybe, while we focus our whole attention on the VIPs and their movements, on peace conferences and protest demonstrations, it's the totally unknown people, praying and working in silence, who make God save us yet again from destruction.

Letters to Marc About Jesus

God's Love Is Stronger Than Death

Even though Jesus went directly against the human inclination to avoid suffering and death, his followers realized that it was better to live the truth with open eyes than to live their lives in illusion [of immortality].

Suffering and death belong to the narrow road of Jesus. Jesus does not glorify them, or call them beautiful, good, or something to be desired. Jesus does not call for heroism or suicidal self-sacrifice. No, Jesus invites us to look at the reality of our existence and reveals this harsh reality as the way to new life. The core message of Jesus is that real joy and peace can never be reached while bypassing suffering and death, but only by going right through them.

We could say: "We really have no choice." Indeed, who escapes suffering and death? Yet there is still a choice. We can deny the reality of life, or we can face it. When we face it not in despair, but with the eyes of Jesus, we discover that where we least expect it, something is hidden that holds a promise stronger than death itself. Jesus lived his life with the trust that God's love is stronger than death and that death, therefore, does not have the last word. He invites us to face the painful reality of our existence with the same trust. This is what Lent is all about.

Show Me the Way

Making Our Deaths Fruitful

What I appreciate as I read Scripture is that Jesus saw death, and his own death in particular, as more than a way of getting from one place to another. He saw his death as potentially fruitful in itself, and of enormous benefit to his disciples. Death was not an ending for him but a passage to something much greater.

When Jesus was anticipating his own death he kept repeating the same theme to his disciples: "My death is good for you, because my death will bear many fruits beyond my death. When I die I will not leave you alone, but I will send you my Spirit, the Paraclete, the Counselor. And my Spirit will reveal to you who I am, what I am teaching you. My Spirit will lead you into the truth and will allow you to have a relationship with me that was not possible before my death. My Spirit will help you to form community and grow in strength." Jesus sees that the real fruits of his life will mature after his death. That is why he adds, "It is good for you that I go."

If that is true, then the real question for me as I consider my own death is not: how much can I still accomplish before I die, or will I be a burden to others? No, the real question is: how can I live so that my death will be fruitful for others? In other words, how can my death be a gift for my loved ones so that they can reap the fruits of my life after I have died? This question can be answered only if I am first willing to admit Jesus' vision of death as a valid possibility for me.

Finding My Way Home

The Fundamental Truth of Your Identity

Jesus died well because he knew he was going to God and he would soon send his Spirit of Love to his friends. "It is good for you that I leave," he said, "because unless I leave, I cannot send my Spirit who will lead you to the full communion, to the full truth, to the full betrothal." With that Holy Spirit he knew that his beloved apostles would live better, happier lives.

This vision is not just about Jesus. It is also about you and me. Jesus came to share his identity with you and to tell you that you are the Beloved Sons and Daughters of God. Just for a moment try to enter this enormous mystery that you, like Jesus, are the beloved daughter or the beloved son of God. This is the truth. Furthermore, your belovedness preceded your birth. You were the beloved before your father, mother, brother, sister, or church loved you or hurt you. You are the beloved because you belong to God from all eternity.

God loved you before you were born, and God will love you after you die. In Scripture, God says, "I have loved you with an everlasting love." This is a very fundamental truth of your identity. This is who you are whether you feel it or not. You belong to God from eternity to eternity. Life is just a little opportunity for you during a few years to say, "I love you, too."

Finding My Way Home

We Are on a Journey

Where are we going? After a very short visit to earth the time comes for each of us to pass from this world to the next. We have been sent into the world as God's beloved children, and in our passages and our losses we learn to love each other as spouse, parent, brother, or sister. We support one another through the passages of life, and together we grow in love. Finally, we ourselves are called to exodus, and we leave the world for full communion with God. It is possible for us, like Jesus, to send our spirit of love to our friends when we leave them. Our spirit, the love we leave behind, is deeply in God's Spirit. It is our greatest gift to those we love.

We, like Jesus, are on a journey, living to make our lives abundantly fruitful through our leaving. When we leave, we will say the words that Jesus said: "It is good for you that I leave, because unless I pass away, I cannot send you my spirit to help you and inspire you."

Finding My Way Home

A Prayer

Dear Lord,

Help me keep my eyes on you. You are the incarnation of Divine Love, you are the expression of God's infinite compassion, you are the visible manifestation of the Father's holiness. You are beauty, goodness, gentleness, forgiveness, and mercy. In you all can be found. Outside of you nothing can be found. Why should I look elsewhere or go elsewhere? You have the words of eternal life, you are food and drink, you are the Way, the Truth, and the Life. You are the light that shines in the darkness, the lamp on the lampstand, the house on the hilltop. You are the perfect Icon of God. In and through you I can see the Heavenly Father, and with you I can find my way to him. O Holy One, Beautiful One, Glorious One, be my Lord, my Savior, my Redeemer, my Guide, my Consoler, my Comforter, my Hope, my Joy, and my Peace. To you I want to give all that I am. Let me be generous, not stingy or hesitant. Let me give you all—all that I have, think, do, and feel. It is yours, O Lord. Please accept it and make it fully your own.

Amen.

A Cry for Mercy

APRIL

God's Non-Violent Love

On the cross, Jesus has shown us how far God's love goes. It's a love that embraces even those who crucified him. When Jesus is hanging nailed to the cross, totally broken and stripped of everything, he still prays for his executioners: "Father, forgive them; they do not know what they are doing." Jesus' love for his enemies knows no bounds. He prays even for those who are putting him to death. It is this, the enemy-loving God, that is offered to us in the Eucharist. To forgive our enemies doesn't lie within our power. That is a divine gift. That's why it's so important to make the Eucharist the heart and center of your life. It's there that you receive the love that empowers you to take the way that Jesus has taken before you: a narrow way, a painful way, but the way that gives you true joy and peace and enables you to make the non-violent love of God visible in this world.

Letters to Marc About Jesus

God's Faithfulness

The resurrection does not solve our problems about dying and death. It is not the happy ending to our life's struggle, nor is it the big surprise that God has kept in store for us. No, the resurrection is the expression of God's faithfulness to Jesus and to all God's children. Through the resurrection, God has said to Jesus, "You are indeed my beloved Son, and my love is everlasting," and to us God has said, "You indeed are my beloved children, and my love is everlasting." The resurrection is God's way of revealing to us that nothing that belongs to God will ever go to waste. What belongs to God will never get lost— not even our mortal bodies. The resurrection doesn't answer any of our curious questions about life after death, such as: How will it be? How will it look? But it does reveal to us that, indeed, love is stronger than death. After that revelation, we must remain silent, leave the whys, wheres, hows, and whens behind, and simply trust.

Our Greatest Gift

God Is a God of the Living

The mystery of God's love is not that our pain is taken away, but that God first wants to share that pain with us. Out of this divine solidarity comes new life. Jesus' being moved in the center of his being by human pain is indeed a movement toward new life. God is our God, the God of the living. In the divine womb of God, life is always born again. . . . The truly good news is that God is not a distant God, a God to be feared and avoided, a God of revenge, but a God who is moved by our pains and participates in the fullness of the human struggle.

Compassion

The Many Rays of Hope

The Easter season is a time of hope. There still is fear, there still is a painful awareness of sinfulness, but there also is light breaking through. Something new is happening, something that goes beyond the changing moods of our life. We can be joyful or sad, optimistic or pessimistic, tranquil or angry, but the solid stream of God's presence moves deeper than the small waves of our minds and hearts. Easter brings the awareness that God is present even when his presence is not directly noticed. Easter brings the good news that, although things seem to get worse in the world, the Evil One has already been overcome. Easter allows us to affirm that although God seems very distant and although we remain preoccupied with many little things, our Lord walks with us on the road and keeps explaining the Scriptures to us. Thus there are many rays of hope casting their light on our way through life.

A Cry for Mercy

Dare to Claim the First Love

The spiritual life starts at the place where you can hear God's voice. Where somehow you can claim that long before your father, your mother, your brother, your sister, your school, your church touched you, loved you, and wounded you—long before that, you were held safe in an eternal embrace. You were seen with eyes of perfect love long before you entered into the dark valley of life.

The spiritual life starts at the moment that you can go beyond all of the wounds and claim that there was a love that was perfect and unlimited, long before that perfect love became reflected in the imperfect and limited, conditional love of people.

The spiritual life starts where you dare to claim the first love. "Love one another because I have loved you first" (see John 4:19).

"Deepening a Prayer Life"

Come Home to Where Love Dwells

The first love says: "You are loved long before other people can love you or you can love others. You are accepted long before you can accept others or receive their acceptance. You are safe long before you can offer or receive safety." Home is the place where that first love dwells and speaks gently to us. It requires discipline to come home and listen, especially when our fears are so noisy that they keep driving us outside of ourselves. But when we grasp the truth that we already have a home, we may at last have the strength to unmask the illusions created by our fears and continue to return again and again and again.

Lifesigns

Claim God's Love for You

For a very long time I considered low self-esteem to be some kind of virtue. I had been warned so often against pride and conceit that I came to consider it a good thing to deprecate myself. But now I realize that the real sin is to deny God's first love for me, to ignore my original goodness. Because without claiming that first love and that original goodness for myself, I lose touch with my true self and embark on the destructive search among the wrong people and in the wrong places for what can only be found in the house of my Father.

The Return of the Prodigal Son

Solidarity Is the Other Side of Intimacy

Those who have entered deeply into their hearts and found the intimate home where they encounter their Lord come to the mysterious discovery that solidarity is the other side of intimacy. They come to the awareness that the intimacy of God's house excludes no one and includes everyone. They start to see that the home they have found in their innermost being is as wide as the whole of humanity. . . . It is of great importance to see the inner connection between intimacy and solidarity. If we fail to recognize this connection, our spirituality will become either privatized or narrowly activist and will no longer reflect the full beauty of living in God's house.

Lifesigns

Do You Own Your Own Pain?

The main question is: "Do you own your pain?" As long as you do not own your pain—that is, integrate your pain into your way of being in the world—the danger exists that you will use the other to seek healing for yourself. When you speak to others about your pain without fully owning it, you expect something from them that they cannot give. As a result, you will feel frustrated, and those you wanted to help will feel confused, disappointed, or even further burdened.

But when you fully own your pain and do not expect those to whom you minister to alleviate it, you can speak about it in true freedom. Then sharing your struggle can become a service; then your openness about yourself can offer courage and hope to others.

The Inner Voice of Love

Distinguish Your Pain from the Pain of Others

There is a real pain in your heart, a pain that truly belongs to you. You know now that you cannot avoid, ignore, or repress it. It is this pain that reveals to you how you are called to live in solidarity with the broken human race.

You must distinguish carefully, however, between your pain and the pains that have attached themselves to your heart but are not truly yours. When you feel rejected, when you think of yourself as a failure and a misfit, you must be careful not to let these feelings and thoughts pierce your heart. You are not a failure or a misfit. Therefore, you have to disown these pains as false. They can paralyze you and prevent you from loving the way you are called to love.

It is a struggle to keep distinguishing the real pain from the false pains. But as you are faithful to that struggle, you will see more and more clearly your unique call to love. As you see that call, you will be more and more able to claim your real pain as your unique way to glory.

The Inner Voice of Love

Jesus Heals Our Pains

How are we healed of our wounding memories? We are healed first of all by letting them be available, by leading them out of the corner of forgetfulness, and by remembering them as part of our life stories. What is forgotten is unavailable and what is unavailable cannot be healed. . . .

By lifting our painful forgotten memories out of the egocentric, individualistic, private sphere, Jesus Christ heals our pains. He connects them with the pain of all humanity, a pain he took upon himself and transformed. To heal, then, does not primarily mean to take pains away but to reveal that our pains are part of a great pain, that our sorrows are part of a great sorrow, that our experience is part of the great experience of him who said, "But was it not ordained that the Christ should suffer and so enter into the Glory of God?" (Luke 24:26).

The Living Reminder

God's Love Casts Out All Fears

Our inclination is to show our Lord only what we feel comfortable with. But the more we dare to reveal our whole trembling self to him, the more we will be able to sense that his love, which is perfect love, casts out all our fears.

Therefore, Lord, I promise I will not run away, not give up, not stop praying, even when it all seems useless, pointless, and a waste of time and effort. I want to let you know that I love you even though I do not feel loved by you, and that I hope in you even though I often experience despair. Let this be a little dying I can do with you and for you as a way of experiencing some solidarity with the millions in this world who suffer far more than I do.

A Cry for Mercy

Trust Unreservedly That You Are Loved

The word *faith* is often understood as accepting something you can't understand. People often say: "Such and such can't be explained, you simply have to believe it." However, when Jesus talks about faith, he means first of all to trust unreservedly that you are loved, so that you can abandon every false way of obtaining love. That's why Jesus tells Nicodemus that, through faith in the descending love of God, we will be set free from anxiety and violence and will find eternal life. It's a question here of trusting in God's love. The Greek word for faith is *pistis,* which means, literally, "trust." Whenever Jesus says to people he has healed: "Your faith has saved you," he is saying that they have found new life because they have surrendered in complete trust to the love of God revealed in him.

Letters to Marc About Jesus

Everything Good Comes from God

Trusting in the unconditional love of God: that is the way to which Jesus calls us. The more firmly you grasp this, the more readily will you be able to perceive why there is so much suspicion, jealousy, bitterness, vindictiveness, hatred, violence, and discord in our world. Jesus himself interprets this by comparing God's love to the light. He says:

Though the light has come into the world
people have preferred
darkness to light
because their deeds were evil.
And indeed, everybody who does wrong
hates the light and avoids it,
to prevent his actions from being shown up;
but whoever does the truth
comes out into the light, so that what he is doing may
    plainly appear as
done in God.

Jesus sees the evil in this world as a lack of trust in God's love. He makes us see that we persistently fall back on ourselves, rely more on ourselves than on God, and are inclined more to love of self than love of God. So we remain in darkness. If we walk in the light, then we are enabled to acknowledge that everything good, beautiful, and true comes from God and is offered to us in love.

Letters to Marc About Jesus

God Is Not a Feeling

Just as God cannot be "caught" or "comprehended" in any specific idea, concept, opinion, or conviction, he cannot be defined by any specific feeling or emotion either. God cannot be identified with a good affectionate feeling toward our neighbor, or with a sweet emotion of the heart or with ecstasies, movements of the body, or handling of snakes. God is not just our good inclinations, our fervor, our generosity, or our love. All these experiences of the heart may remind us of God's presence, but their absence does not prove God's absence. God is not only greater than our mind; he is also greater than our heart, and just as we have to avoid the temptation of adapting God to our small concepts we also have to avoid adapting him to our small feelings.

Reaching Out

Obstacles to God's Love

What keeps us from opening to the reality of the world? Could it be that we cannot accept our powerlessness and are only willing to see those wounds that we can heal? Could it be that we do not want to give up our illusion that we are masters over our world and, therefore, create our own Disneyland where we can make ourselves believe that all events of life are safely under control? Could it be that our blindness and deafness are signs of our own resistance to acknowledging that we are not the Lord of the Universe? It is hard to allow these questions to go beyond the level of rhetoric and to really sense in our innermost self how much we resent our powerlessness. . . .

The astonishing thing is that the battle for survival has become so "normal" that few people really believe that it can be different. . . . Oh, how important is discipline, community, prayer, silence, caring presence, simple listening, adoration, and deep, lasting faithful friendship. We all want it so much, and still the powers suggesting that all of that is fantasy are enormous. But we have to replace the battle for power with the battle to create space for the spirit.

Reaching Out; The Road to Daybreak

Jesus Makes Our Deepest Self Known

Our heart is at the center of our being human. There our deepest thoughts, intuitions, emotions, and decisions find their source. But it's also there that we are often most alienated from ourselves. We know little or nothing of our own heart. We keep our distance, as though we were afraid of it. What is most intimate is also what frightens us most. Where we are most ourselves, we are often strangers to ourselves. That is the painful part of our being human. We fail to know our hidden center; and so we live and die often without knowing who we really are. If we ask ourselves why we think, feel, and act in such and such a way, we often have no answer, thus proving to be strangers in our own house.

The mystery of the spiritual life is that Jesus desires to meet us in the seclusion of our own heart, to make his love known to us there, to free us from our fears, and to make our own deepest self known to us. In the privacy of our heart, therefore, we can learn not only to know Jesus but, through Jesus, ourselves as well.

Letters to Marc About Jesus

The Heart Is the Seat of Prayer

In our milieu the word *heart* has become a soft word. It refers to the seat of a sentimental life. Expressions such as "heartbroken" and "heartfelt" show that we often think of the heart as the warm place where the emotions are located in contrast to the cool intellect where our thoughts find their home. But the word *heart* in the Jewish-Christian tradition refers to the source of all physical, emotional, intellectual, volitional, and moral energies.

From the heart arise unknowable impulses as well as conscious feelings, moods, and wishes. The heart, too, has its reasons and is the center of perception and understanding. Finally, the heart is the seat of the will: it makes plans and comes to good decisions. Thus the heart is the central and unifying organ of our personal life. Our heart determines our personality, and is, therefore, not only the place where God dwells but also the place to which Satan directs his fiercest attacks. It is this heart that is the place of prayer. The prayer of the heart is a prayer that directs itself to God from the center of the person and thus affects the whole of our humanness.

The Way of the Heart

We Meet the World with a Heart at Rest

The prayer of the heart is indeed the way to the purity of heart that gives us eyes to see the reality of our existence. This purity of heart allows us to see more clearly, not only our own needy, distorted, and anxious self but also the caring face of our compassionate God. When that vision remains clear and sharp, it will be possible to move into the midst of a tumultuous world with a heart at rest. It is this restful heart that will attract those who are groping to find their way through life. When we have found our rest in God we can do nothing other than minister. God's rest will be visible wherever we go and to whomever we meet. And before we speak any words, the Spirit of God, praying in us, will make his presence known and gather people into a new body, the body of Christ himself.

The Way of the Heart

Prayer Is Grace

We cannot force God into a relationship. God comes to us on his own initiative, and no discipline, effort, or ascetic practice can make him come. All mystics stress with an impressive unanimity that prayer is "grace"—that is, a free gift from God, to which we can only respond with gratitude. But they hasten to add that this precious gift indeed is within our reach. In Jesus Christ, God has entered into our lives in the most intimate way, so that we could enter into his life through the Spirit.

Reaching Out

Descend into the Heart

The quiet repetition of a single word can help us to descend with the mind into the heart. This repetition has nothing to do with magic. It's not meant to throw a spell on God or to force him into hearing us. On the contrary, a word or sentence repeated frequently can help us to concentrate, to move to the center, to create an inner stillness, and thus to listen to the voice of God. When we simply try to sit silently and wait for God to speak to us, we find ourselves bombarded with endless conflicting thoughts and ideas. But when we use a very simple sentence such as "O God, come to my assistance," or "Jesus, master, have mercy on me," or a word such as "Lord" or "Jesus," it is easier to let the many distractions pass by without being misled by them. Such a simple, easily repeated prayer can slowly empty out our crowded interior life and create the quiet space where we can dwell with God. It can be like a ladder along which we can descend into the heart and ascend to God.

The Way of the Heart

Stay Awake

The practice of contemplative prayer is the discipline by which we begin to "see" the living God dwelling in our own hearts. Careful attentiveness to the One who makes a home in the privileged center of our being gradually leads to recognition. As we come to know and love the Father of our hearts we give ourselves over to this incredible Presence who takes possession of all our senses. By the discipline of prayer we are awakened and opened to God within, who enters into our heartbeat and our breathing, into our thoughts and emotions, our hearing, seeing, touching, and tasting. It is by being awake to this God within that we also find the Presence in the world around us. Here we are again in front of the secret. It is not that we see God in the world, but that God-with-us recognizes God in the world. God speaks to God, Spirit speaks to Spirit, heart speaks to heart.

Contemplation, therefore, is a participating in the divine self-recognition. The divine Spirit alive in us makes our world transparent for us and opens our eyes to the presence of the divine Spirit in all that surrounds us. It is with our heart of hearts that we see the heart of the world. . . .

Clowning in Rome

In Prayer We Present Our Thoughts to God

To pray, I think, does not mean to think about God in contrast to thinking about other things, nor does it mean spending time with God instead of spending time with other people. As soon as we begin to divide our thoughts into thoughts about God and thoughts about other things, like people and events, we separate God from our daily life. At that point God is allocated to a pious little niche in some corner of our lives where we only think pious thoughts and experience pious feelings. Although it is important and even indispensable for our spiritual lives to set apart time for God and God alone, our prayer can only become unceasing [prayer] when all our thoughts—beautiful or ugly, high or low, proud or shameful, sorrowful or joyful—can be thought in the presence of the One who dwells in us and surrounds us. By trying to do this, our unceasing thinking is converted into unceasing prayer, moving us from a self-centered monologue to a God-centered dialogue. To do this we want to try to convert our thoughts into conversation. The main question, therefore, is not so much what we think, but to whom we present our thoughts.

Clowning in Rome

Solitude Creates Space for God

To live a Christian life means to live in the world without being of it. It is in solitude that this inner freedom can grow. Jesus went to a lonely place to pray, that is, to grow in the awareness that all the power he had was given to him; that all the words he spoke came from his Father; and that all the works he did were not really his but the works of the One who had sent him. In the lonely place Jesus was made free to fail.

A life without a lonely place, that is, a life without a quiet center, easily becomes destructive. When we cling to the results of our actions as our only way of self-identification, then we become possessive and defensive and tend to look at our fellow human beings more as enemies to be kept at a distance than as friends with whom we share the gifts of life.

In solitude we can slowly unmask the illusion of our possessiveness and discover in the center of our own self that we are not what we can conquer, but what is given to us. In solitude we can listen to the voice of him who spoke to us before we could speak a word, who healed us before we could make any gesture to help, who set us free long before we could free others, and who loved us long before we could give love to anyone. It is in this solitude that we discover that being is more important than having, and that we are worth more than the results of our efforts. In solitude we discover that our life is not a possession to be defended, but a gift to be shared. It's there we recognize that the healing words we speak are not just our own, but are given to us; that the love we can express is part of a greater love; and the new life we bring forth is not a property to cling to, but a gift to be received.

Out of Solitude

God's Absence and Presence

God is "beyond," beyond our heart and mind, beyond our feelings and thoughts, beyond our expectations and desires, and beyond all the events and experiences that make up our life. Still God is in the center of all of it. Here we touch the heart of prayer, since here it becomes manifest that in prayer the distinction between God's presence and God's absence no longer really distinguishes. In prayer, God's presence is never separated from God's absence and God's absence is never separated from God's presence. God's presence is so much beyond the human experience of being together that it quite easily is perceived as absence. God's absence, on the other hand, is often so deeply felt that it leads to a new sense of God's presence. . . .

"My God, my God, why have you deserted me?" (Psalms 22:1). . . . When Jesus spoke these words on the cross, total aloneness and full acceptance touched each other. In that moment of complete emptiness all was fulfilled. In that hour of darkness new light was seen. While death was witnessed, life was affirmed. Where God's absence was most loudly expressed, God's presence was most profoundly revealed. When God, through the humanity of Jesus, freely chose to share our own most painful experience of divine absence, God became most present to us. It is into this mystery that we enter when we pray.

Reaching Out

God Is Gentle

While realizing that ten years ago I didn't have the faintest idea that I would end up where I am now, I still like to keep up the illusion that I am in control of my own life. I like to decide what I most need, what I will do next, what I want to accomplish, and how others will think of me. While being so busy running my own life, I become oblivious to the gentle movements of the Spirit of God within me, pointing me in directions quite different from my own.

It requires a lot of inner solitude and silence to become aware of these divine movements. God does not shout, scream, or push. The Spirit of God is soft and gentle like a small voice or a light breeze. It is the Spirit of Love.

Here and Now

Open Yourself to God

To pray means to open your hands before God. It means slowly relaxing the tension that squeezes your hands together and accepting your existence with an increasing readiness, not as a possession to defend, but as a gift to receive. Above all, prayer is a way of life that allows you to find stillness in the midst of the world where you open your hands to God's promises and find hope for yourself, your neighbor, and your world. In prayer, you encounter God not only in the small voice and the soft breeze, but also in the midst of the turmoil of the world, in the distress and joy of your neighbor, and in the loneliness of your own heart.

Prayer leads you to see new paths and to hear new melodies in the air. Prayer is the breath of your life that gives you freedom to go and to stay where you wish, to find the many signs that point out the way to a new land. Praying is not simply some necessary compartment in the daily schedule of a Christian or a source of support in a time of need, nor is it restricted to Sunday mornings or mealtimes. Praying is living. It is eating and drinking, acting and resting, teaching and learning, playing and working. Praying pervades every aspect of our lives. It is the unceasing recognition that God is wherever we are, always inviting us to come closer and to celebrate the divine gift of being alive.

In the end, a life of prayer is a life with open hands—a life where we need not be ashamed of our weaknesses but realize that it is more perfect for us to be led by the Other than to try to hold everything in our own hands.

With Open Hands

28

The Kingdom of God Is Within You

The Jesus Prayer,* or any other prayer form, is meant to be a help to gently empty our minds from all that is not God, and offer all the room to him and him alone. But that is not all. Our prayer becomes a prayer of the heart when we have localized in the center of our inner being the empty space in which our God-filled mind can descend and vanish, and where the distinctions between thinking and feeling, knowing and experience, ideas and emotions are transcended, and where God can become our host. "The Kingdom of God is within you" (Luke 17:21), Jesus said. The prayer of the heart takes these words seriously. When we empty our minds from all thoughts and our hearts from all experiences, we can prepare in the center of our innermost being the home for the God who wants to dwell in us. Then we can say with St. Paul, "I live now not with my own life but with the life of Christ who lives in me" (Galatians 2:20). Then we can affirm Luther's words, "Grace is the experience of being delivered from experience." And then we can realize that it is not we who pray, but the Spirit of God who prays in us.

Reaching Out

---

* See footnote on March 18.

Create Space in Your Innermost Self

Today I imagined my inner self as a place crowded with pins and needles. How could I receive anyone in my prayer when there is no place for them to be free and relaxed? When I am still so full of preoccupations, jealousies, angry feelings, anyone who enters will get hurt. I had a very vivid realization that I must create some free space in my innermost self so that I may indeed invite others to enter and be healed. To pray for others means to offer others a hospitable place where I can really listen to their needs and pains. Compassion, therefore, calls for a self-scrutiny that can lead to inner gentleness.

The Genesee Diary

A Prayer

Dear God,

I am so afraid to open my clenched fists!
Who will I be when I have nothing left to hold on to?
Who will I be when I stand before you with empty hands?
Please help me to gradually open my hands
and to discover that I am not what I own,
but what you want to give me.
And what you want to give me is love—
unconditional, everlasting love.

Amen.

With Open Hands

MAY

Clear the Path to Your Heart

To be calm and quiet by yourself is not the same as sleeping. In fact, it means being fully awake and following with close attention every move going on inside of you. It requires the discipline to recognize the urge to get up and go as a temptation to look elsewhere for what is really close at hand. It offers the freedom to stroll through your own inner yard and rake up the leaves and clear the path so you can easily find the way to your heart. Perhaps there will be fear and uncertainty when you first come upon this "unfamiliar terrain," but slowly and surely you will discover an order and a familiarity that deepens your longing to stay home with yourself.

With Open Hands

The Spirit of God Prays in Us

Silence means rest, rest of body and mind in which we become available for him whose heart is greater than ours. That is very threatening; it is like giving up control over our actions and thoughts, allowing something creative to happen not by us but to us. Is it so amazing that we are so often tired and exhausted, trying to be masters of ourselves, wanting to grasp the ultimate meaning of our existence, struggling with our identity? Silence is that moment in which we not only stop the discussion with others but also the inner discussions with ourselves, in which we can breathe in freely and accept our identity as a gift. "Not I live, but He lives in me." It is in this silence that the Spirit of God can pray in us and continue his creative work in us. . . . Without silence the Spirit will die in us and the creative energy of our life will float away and leave us alone, cold, and tired. Without silence we will lose our center and become the victim of the many who constantly demand our attention.

Intimacy

Expect God's Secret

Deep silence leads us to realize that prayer is, above all, acceptance. When we pray, we are standing with our hands open to the world. We know that God will become known to us in the nature around us, in people we meet, and in situations we run into. We trust that the world holds God's secret within and we expect that secret to be shown to us. Prayer creates that openness in which God is given to us. Indeed, God wants to be admitted into the human heart, received with open hands, and loved with the same love with which we have been created.

With Open Hands

"Waste" Your Time with God

John Eudes* talked about that moment, that point, that lies before comparison, before the beginning of the vicious cycle or the self-fulfilling prophecy. That is the moment, point, or place where meditation can enter in. It is the moment to stop reading, speaking, socializing, and to "waste" your time in meditation. When you find your mind competing again, you might plan an "empty time" of meditation, in this way interrupting the vicious circle of your ruminations and entering into the depth of your own soul. There you can be with him who was before you came, who loved you before you could love, and has given you your own self before any comparison was possible. In meditation we can come to the affirmation that we are not created by other people but by God, that we are not judged by how we compare with others but by how we fulfill the will of God.

The Genesee Diary

---

* Dom John Eudes Bamberger, O.C.S.O. was Henri's spiritual advisor at the Abbey of the Genesee, where Henri was a temporary Trappist monk for seven months in the 1970s.

See Through Things

Contemplative life is a human response to the fundamental fact that the central things in life, although spiritually perceptible, remain invisible in large measure and can very easily be overlooked by the inattentive, busy, distracted person that each of us can so readily become. The contemplative looks not so much around things but through them into their center. Through their center he discovers the world of spiritual beauty that is more real, has more density, more mass, more energy, and greater intensity than physical matter. In effect, the beauty of physical matter is a reflection of its inner content.

The Genesee Diary

Keep Your Eyes Fixed on Jesus

K eep your eyes fixed on Jesus and ask him more directly to give you joy, peace, and a pure heart. Purity of heart means a heart where God is the center of your attention. Take a simple sentence like "The Lord is my shepherd there is nothing I shall want," and repeat that quietly during the day until the truth of it enters the center of your being. You will always continue to have feelings of depression, anger, and restlessness, but when God dwells in the center of the storm, the storm is less frightening and you can live with trust that in the midst of all of the darkness you will be led to a place of joy and peace.

Unpublished letter

Meditation Brings Us to the Source of Love

Human withdrawal [for meditation] is a very painful and lonely process, because it forces us to directly face our own condition in all its misery as well as its beauty. But when we are not afraid to enter into our own center and to concentrate on the stirrings of our own souls, we come to know that being alive means being loved. This experience tells us that we can only love because we are born out of love, that we can only give because our life is a gift, and that we can only make others free because we are set free by the One whose heart is greater than ours.

And when we have found the anchor places for our lives in our own center we can be free to let others enter into the space created for them, and allow them to dance their own dance, sing their own song, and speak their own language without fear. Then our presence is no longer threatening and demanding, but inviting and liberating.

The Wounded Healer

When We Have Nothing to Lose

When we feel lonely we have such a need to be liked and loved that we are hypersensitive to the many signals in our environment and easily become hostile toward anyone whom we perceive as rejecting us. But once we have found the center of our life in our own heart and have accepted our aloneness not as a fate but as a vocation, we are able to offer freedom to others. Once we have given up our desire to be fully fulfilled, we can offer emptiness to others. Once we have become poor, we can be a good host. It is indeed the paradox of hospitality that poverty makes a good host. Poverty is the inner disposition that allows us to take away our defenses and convert our enemies into friends. We can only perceive the stranger as an enemy as long as we have something to defend. But when we say, "Please enter—my house is your house, my joy is your joy, my sadness is your sadness, and my life is your life," we have nothing to defend, since we have nothing to lose but all to give.

Reaching Out

Through Prayer We Enter into God's Compassionate Heart

Prayer is far from sweet and easy. Being the expression of our greatest love, it does not keep pain way from us. Instead, it makes us suffer more since our love for God is a love for a suffering God and our entering into God's intimacy is an entering into the intimacy where all of human suffering is embraced in divine compassion. To the degree that our prayer has become the prayer of our heart we will love more and suffer more, we will see more light and more darkness, more grace and more sin, more of God and more of humanity. To the degree that we have descended into our heart and reached out to God from there, solitude can speak to solitude, deep to deep, and heart to heart. It is there where love and pain are found together.

Reaching Out

You Are the Glory of God

With a smile John Eudes said, "Take this as a koan: 'I am the glory of God.' Make that thought the center of your meditation so that it slowly becomes not only a thought but a living reality. You are the place where God chose to dwell, you are the *topos tou theou* (God's place) and the spiritual life is nothing more or less than to allow that space to exist where God can dwell, to create the space where his glory can manifest itself. In your meditation you can ask yourself, 'Where is the glory of God? If the glory of God is not there where I am, where else can it be?'"

The Genesee Diary

Be Still and Wait

M aybe I have been living much too fast, too restlessly, too feverishly, forgetting to pay attention to what is happening here and now, right under my nose. Just as a whole world of beauty can be discovered in one flower, so the great grace of God can be tasted in one small moment. Just as no great travels are necessary to see the beauty of creation, so no great ecstasies are needed to discover the love of God. But you have to be still and wait so that you can realize that God is not in the earthquake, the storm, or the lightning, but in the gentle breeze with which he touches your back.

The Genesee Diary

Something Has Happened

One of the experiences of prayer is that it seems that nothing happens. But when you stay with it and look back over a long period of prayer, you suddenly realize that something has happened. What is most close, most intimate, most present often cannot be experienced directly but only with a certain distance. When I think I am only distracted, just wasting my time, something is happening too immediate for knowing, understanding, and experiencing. Only in retrospect do I realize that something very important has taken place. Isn't this true of all really important events in life? When I am together with someone I love very much, we seldom talk about our relationship. The relationship, in fact, is too central to be a subject of talk. But later, after we have separated and write letters, we realize how much it all meant to us, and we even write about it.

The Genesee Diary

Let Yourself Be Useless

Prayer is not a way of being busy with God instead of with people. In fact, it unmasks the illusion of busyness, usefulness, and indispensability. It is a way of being empty and useless in the presence of God and so of proclaiming our basic belief that all is grace and nothing is simply the result of hard work. Indeed, wasting time for God is an act of ministry, because it reminds us and our people that God is free to touch anyone regardless of our well-meant efforts. Prayer as an articulate way of being useless in the face of God brings a smile to all we do and creates humor in the midst of our occupations and preoccupations.

Thinking about my own prayer, I realize how easily I make it into a little seminar with God, during which I want to be useful by reading beautiful prayers, thinking profound thoughts, and saying impressive words. I am obviously still worried about the grade! It indeed is a hard discipline to be useless in God's presence and to let him speak in the silence of my heart. But whenever I become a little useless I know that God is calling me to a new life beyond the boundaries of my usefulness.

The Living Reminder

God Invites Us into Unceasing Conversation

Prayer is not introspection. It is not a scrupulous, inward-looking analysis of our own thoughts and feelings but it is a careful attentiveness to the Presence of Love personified inviting us to an encounter. Prayer is the presentation of our thoughts—reflective thoughts, as well as daydreams, and night dreams—to the One who receives them, sees them in the light of unconditional love, and responds to them with divine compassion. This context of thinking in the Presence, of conversation and dialogue with Love, is the joyful affirmation of our gentle Companion on the journey with God who knows our minds and hearts, our goodness and our beauty, our darkness and our light. The Psalmist prays the prayer for us (Psalms 139:1–3; 23–24):

> O Lord, you search me and you know me,
> you know my resting and my rising,
> you discern my purpose from afar.
> You mark when I walk or lie down,
> all my ways lie open to you. . . .
> O search me, God, and know my heart.
> O test me and know my thoughts.
> See that I follow not the wrong path
> and lead me in the path of life eternal.

Clowning in Rome

Imagining Christ

Contemplative prayer can be described as an imagining of God's Son, Jesus, a letting him enter fully into our consciousness so that he becomes the icon always present in the inner room of our hearts. By gazing at Jesus, walking on the earth, we give him loving attention and we "see" with our minds and hearts how he is the way to the Father. Jesus' life and work is an uninterrupted union with and contemplation of his Father. We, as followers of Jesus, try to enter into the same disposition. We welcome the discipline of contemplation, taking time regularly to enter into the life of Jesus to contemplate the incredible bond between Jesus and the Father. And we trust that in, through, and with Jesus, we, too, may live and bask in God's unconditional love.

Clowning in Rome

The Word of God Remains Forever

The grass withers, the flower fades, but the word of our God remains for ever" (Isaiah 40:8). The Word of God is powerful indeed. Not only the Jesus Prayer* but many words from the Scriptures can reshape the inner self. When I take the words that strike me during a service into the day and slowly repeat them while reading or working, more or less chewing on them, they create new life. Sometimes when I wake up during the night I am still saying them, and they become like wings carrying me above the moods and turbulences of the days and weeks.

The Genesee Diary

* See footnote on March 18.

We Become What We Imagine

When I bring myself into the presence of God, I imagine him in many ways: as a loving father, a supporting sister, a caring mother, a severe teacher, an honest judge, a fellow traveler, an intimate friend, a gentle healer, a challenging leader, a demanding taskmaster. All these "personalities" create images in my mind that affect not only what I think, but also what I actually experience myself. I believe that true prayer makes us into what we imagine. To pray to God leads to becoming like God. . . .

The more we come to depend on the images offered to us by those who try to distract us, entertain us, use us for their purposes, and make us conform to the demands of a consumer society, the easier it is for us to lose our identity. These imposed images actually make us into the world that they represent, a world of hatred, violence, lust, greed, manipulations, and oppression. But when we believe that we are created in the image of God himself and come to realize that Christ came to let us reimagine this, then meditation and prayer can lead us to our true identity.

Gracias!

Listen to the Voice of Gentle Love

L isten to your heart. It's there that Jesus speaks most intimately to you. Praying is first and foremost listening to Jesus who dwells in the very depths of your heart. He doesn't shout. He doesn't thrust himself upon you. His voice is an unassuming voice, very nearly a whisper, the voice of a gentle love. Whatever you do with your life, go on listening to the voice of Jesus in your heart. This listening must be an active and very attentive listening, for in our restless and noisy world God's so loving voice is easily drowned out. You need to set aside some time every day for this active listening to God if only for ten minutes. Ten minutes each day for Jesus alone can bring about a radical change in your life.

You'll find it isn't easy to be still for ten minutes at a time. You'll discover straightaway that many other voices, voices that are very noisy and distracting, voices that do not come from God, demand your attention. But if you stick to your daily prayer time, then slowly but surely you'll come to hear the gentle voice of love and will long more and more to listen to it.

Letters to Marc About Jesus

Forgive Your Enemies

Christians mention one another in their prayers (Romans 1:9; 2 Corinthians 1:11; Ephesians 6:8; Colossians 4:3), and in so doing they bring help and even salvation to those for whom they pray (Romans 15:30; Philippians 1:19). But the final test of compassionate prayer goes beyond prayers for fellow Christians, members of the community, friends, and relatives. Jesus says it most unambiguously, "I say this to you: love your enemies and pray for those who persecute you" (Matthew 5:44); and in the depth of his agony on the cross, he prays for those who are killing him, "Father, forgive them; they do not know what they are doing" (Luke 23:34). Here the full significance of the discipline of prayer becomes visible. Prayer allows us to lead into the center of our hearts not only those who love us but also those who hate us. This is possible only when we are willing to make our enemies part of ourselves and thus convert them first of all in our own hearts.

Compassion

Prayer Is to Be Shared

M uch that has been said about prayer might create the false impression that prayer is a private, individualistic, and nearly secret affair, so personal and so deeply hidden in our inner life that it can hardly be talked about, even less be shared. The opposite is true. Just because prayer is so personal and arises from the center of our life, it is to be shared with others. Just because prayer is the most precious expression of being human, it needs the constant support and protection of the community to grow and flower. Just because prayer is our highest vocation, needing careful attention and faithful perseverance, we cannot allow it to be a private affair. Just because prayer asks for a patient waiting in expectation, it should never become the most individualistic expression of the most individualistic emotion, but should always remain embedded in the life of the community of which we are part.

Reaching Out

Community Is Heart Calling to Heart

Friendship, marriage, family, religious life, and every other form of community is solitude greeting solitude, spirit speaking to spirit, and heart calling to heart. It is the grateful recognition of God's call to share life together and the joyful offering of a hospitable space where the re-creating power of God's Spirit can become manifest. Thus all forms of life together can become ways to reveal to each other the real presence of God in our midst.

Community has little to do with mutual compatibility. Similarities in educational background, psychological makeup, or social status can bring us together, but they can never be the basis for community. Community is grounded in God, who calls us together, and not in the attractiveness of people to each other. . . . The mystery of community is precisely that it embraces all people, whatever their individual differences may be, and allows them to live together as brothers and sisters of Christ and sons and daughters of his heavenly Father.

Making All Things New

Community Is a Quality of the Heart

The search for community is a deeply human search and I have felt that the ideal community remains mostly the object of my hopes and dreams. But I have also experienced that if I keep those hopes and dreams alive, true community will reveal itself in the most unexpected places and times. Somehow, community is first of all a quality of the heart, a quality that touches all those whom you meet in your life, not only your own family, but also the people you work and play with.

The source of all community, however, is your most intimate relationship with the Lord because the deeper you enter into communion with him, the more clearly you will find that all those whom you love are hidden in his heart. This truth does not solve all our pains and problems, but it certainly can set us free at times to travel on and to move forward even though our emotions can make us feel very lonely.

Keep close to the Bible and taste it to the full. There is a very deep hunger in many people for the life in the Spirit and many people need to be nurtured continuously by the Word of God.

Unpublished letter

We Are Windows to God's Love

The discipline of community makes us persons; that is, people who are sounding through to each other (the Latin *personare* means "sounding through") a truth, a beauty, and a love that is greater, fuller, and richer than we ourselves can grasp. In true community we are windows constantly offering each other new views on the mystery of God's presence in our lives. Thus the discipline of community is a true discipline of prayer. It makes us alert to the presence of the Spirit who cries out "Abba," Father, among us and thus prays from the center of our common life. Community thus is obedience practiced together. The question is not simply "Where does God lead me as an individual person who tried to do his will?" More basic and more significant is the question "Where does God lead us as a people?"

Making All Things New

Together We Pray to God

Prayer is the language of the Christian community. In prayer the nature of the community becomes visible because in prayer we direct ourselves to the One who forms the community. We do not pray to each other, but together we pray to God, who calls us and makes us into a new people. Praying is not one of the many things the community does. Rather, it is its very being. Many discussions about prayer do not take this very seriously. Sometimes it seems as if the Christian community is "so busy" with its projects and plans that there is neither the time nor the mood to pray. But when prayer is no longer its primary concern, and when its many activities are no longer seen and experienced as part of prayer itself, the community quickly degenerates into a club with a common cause but no common vocation.

By prayer, community is created as well as expressed. Prayer is first of all the realization of the community itself. Most clear and most noticeable are the words, the gestures, and the silence through which the community is formed. When we listen to the word, we not only receive insight into God's saving work, but we also experience a new mutual bond. When we stand around the altar, eat bread and drink wine, kneel in meditation, or walk in procession, we not only remember God's work in human history, but we also become aware of God's creative presence here and now. When we sit together in silent prayer, we create a space where we sense that the One we are waiting for is already touching us, as he touched Elijah in front of the cave (1 Kings 19:13).

Reaching Out

God Is with Us in Community

The community of faith offers the protective boundaries within which we can listen to our deepest longings, not to indulge in morbid introspection, but to find our God to whom they point. In the community of faith we can listen to our feelings of loneliness, to our desires for an embrace or a kiss, to our sexual urges, to our cravings for sympathy, compassion, or just a good word; also to our search for insight and to our hope for companionship and friendship. In the community of faith we can listen to all these longings and find the courage, not to avoid them or cover them up, but to confront them in order to discern God's presence in their midst.

Reaching Out

Prayer Leads to Compassion

Prayer and action can never be seen as contradictory or mutually exclusive. Prayer without action grows into powerless pietism, and action without prayer degenerates into questionable manipulation. If prayer leads us into deeper unity with the compassionate Christ, it will always give rise to concrete acts of service. And if concrete acts of service do indeed lead us to a deeper solidarity with the poor, the hungry, the sick, the dying, and the oppressed, they will always give rise to prayer. In prayer we meet Christ, and in him all human suffering. In service we meet people, and in them the suffering Christ. . . .

Action with and for those who suffer is the concrete expression of a compassionate life and the final criterion of being a Christian. Such acts do not stand beside the moments of prayer and worship but are themselves such moments. Why? Because Jesus Christ, who did not cling to his divinity, but became as we are, can be found where there are hungry, thirsty, alienated, naked, sick, and imprisoned people. Precisely when we live in an ongoing conversation with Christ and allow the Spirit to guide our lives, we will recognize Christ in the poor, the oppressed, and the downtrodden and will hear his cry and respond to it wherever he is revealed.

Compassion

We Can Live Free, Joyful, Courageous Lives

The Holy Spirit, whom Jesus promised to his followers, is the great gift of God. Without the Spirit of Jesus we can do nothing, but in and through his Spirit we can live free, joyful, and courageous lives. We cannot pray, but the Spirit of Christ can pray in us. We cannot create peace and joy, but the Spirit of Christ can fill us with a peace and joy that is not of this world. We cannot break through the many barriers that divide races, sexes, and nations, but the Spirit of Christ unites all people in the all-embracing love of God. The Spirit of Christ burns away our many fears and anxieties and sets us free to move wherever we are sent. That is the great liberation of Pentecost.

A Cry for Mercy

Be Alone with God

S olitude and silence can never be separated from the call to
unceasing prayer. If solitude were primarily an escape from
a busy joy, and silence primarily an escape from a noisy milieu,
they could easily become very self-centered forms of asceticism.
But solitude and silence are for prayer. The Desert Fathers did
not think of solitude as being alone, but as being alone with
God. They did not think of silence as not speaking but as listening to God. Solitude and silence are the context within which
prayer is practiced.

The Way of the Heart

Solitude Is the Place of Conversion

In order to understand the meaning of solitude, we must first unmask the ways in which the idea of solitude has been distorted by our world. We say to each other that we need some solitude in our lives. What we really are thinking of, however, is a time and place for ourselves in which we are not bothered by other people, can think our own thoughts, express our own complaints, and do our own thing, whatever it may be. For us, solitude most often means privacy. We have come to the dubious conviction that we all have a right to privacy. Solitude thus becomes like a spiritual property for which we can compete on the free market of spiritual goods. But there is more. We also think of solitude as a station where we can recharge our batteries, or as a corner of the boxing ring where our wounds are oiled, our muscles massaged, and our courage restored by fitting slogans. In short, we think of solitude as a place where we gather new strength to continue the ongoing competition of life.

But that is not the solitude of St. John the Baptist, of St. Anthony or St. Benedict, of Charles de Foucauld or the brothers of [the] Taizé [Community]. For them solitude is not a private therapeutic place. Rather, it is the place of conversion, the place where the old self dies and the new self is born, the place where the emergence of the new man and the new woman occurs.

The Way of the Heart

Hear the Voice That Calls You the Beloved

Solitude is listening to the voice that calls you the Beloved. It is being alone with the One who says, "You are my Beloved, I want to be with you. Don't go running around, don't start to prove to everybody that you're beloved. You are already beloved." That is what God says to us. Solitude is the place where we go in order to hear the truth about ourselves. It asks us to let go of the other ways of proving, which are a lot more satisfying. The voice that calls us the beloved is not the voice that satisfies the senses. That's what the whole mystical life is about; it is beyond feelings and beyond thoughts.

Beloved: Henri Nouwen in Conversation

A Prayer

Dear God,

Speak gently in my silence.
When the loud outer noises of my surroundings
and the loud inner noises of my fears
keep pulling me away from you,
help me to trust that you are still there
even when I am unable to hear you.
Give me ears to listen to your small, soft voice saying:
"Come to me, you who are overburdened, and I will give you
    rest . . .
for I am gentle and humble of heart."
Let that loving voice be my guide.

Amen.

With Open Hands

JUNE

Joy

J oy is essential to the spiritual life. Whatever we may think of
or say about God, when we are not joyful, our thoughts and
words cannot bear fruit. Jesus reveals to us God's love so that his
joy may become ours and that our joy may become complete.
Joy is the experience of knowing that you are unconditionally
loved and that nothing—sickness, failure, emotional distress,
oppression, war, or even death—can take that love away.

Joy is not the same as happiness. We can be unhappy about
many things, but joy can still be there because it comes from the
knowledge of God's love for us. . . . Joy does not simply happen
to us. We have to choose joy and keep choosing it every day. It
is a choice based on the knowledge that we belong to God and
have found in God our refuge and our safety and that nothing,
not even death, can take God away from us.

Here and Now

Joy and Resentment Cannot Coexist

O f one thing I am sure. Complaining is self-perpetuating and counterproductive. Whenever I express my complaints in the hope of evoking pity and receiving the satisfaction I so much desire, the result is always the opposite of what I tried to get. A complainer is hard to live with, and very few people know how to respond to the complaints made by a self-rejecting person. The tragedy is that, often, the complaint, once expressed, leads to that which is most feared: further rejection. . . . Joy and resentment cannot coexist.

The Return of the Prodigal Son

Joys and Sorrows Kiss

When we speak about celebration we tend rather easily to bring to mind happy, pleasant, gay festivities in which we can forget for a while the hardships of life and immerse ourselves in an atmosphere of music, dance, drinks, laughter, and a lot of cozy small talk. But celebration in the Christian sense has very little to do with this. Celebration is only possible through the deep realization that life and death are never found completely separate. Celebration can only really come about where fear and love, joy and sorrow, tears and smiles can exist together. Celebration is the acceptance of life in a constantly increasing awareness of its preciousness. And life is precious not only because it can be seen, touched, and tasted, but also because it will be gone one day. When we celebrate a wedding, we celebrate a union as well as a departure; when we celebrate death we celebrate lost friendship as well as gained liberty. There can be tears after weddings and smiles after funerals. We can indeed make our sorrows, just as much as our joys, a part of our celebration of life in the deep reality that life and death are not opponents but do, in fact, kiss each other at every moment of our existence.

Creative Ministry

Celebrate in the Present

Celebrating is first of all the full affirmation of our present condition. We say with full consciousness: we are, we are here, we are now, and let it be that way. We can only really celebrate when we are present in the present. If anything has become clear, it is that we have to a large extent lost the capability to live in the present. Many so-called celebrations are not much more than a painful moment between bothersome preparations and boring after-talks. We can only celebrate if there is something present that can be celebrated. We cannot celebrate Christmas when there is nothing new born here and now; we cannot celebrate Easter when no new life becomes visible; we cannot celebrate Pentecost when there is no Spirit whatsoever to celebrate. Celebration is the recognition that something is there and needs to be made visible so that we can all say yes to it.

Creative Ministry

A Current of Joy

Celebration is not just a way to make people feel good for a while; it is the way in which faith in the God of life is lived out, through both laughter and tears. Thus celebration goes beyond ritual, custom, and tradition. It is the unceasing affirmation that underneath all the ups and downs of life there flows a solid current of joy. The handicapped men and women of L'Arche* are becoming my teachers in the most important course of all: living in the house of God. Their joy leads me beyond the fearful place of all death and opens my eyes to the ecstatic potential of all life. Joy offers the solid ground from which new life can always burst. Joy can be caught neither in one feeling or emotion nor in one ritual or custom but is always more than we expect, always surprising, and, therefore, always a sign that we are in the presence of the Lord of life.

Lifesigns

---

* L'Arche is an International Federation dedicated to the creation and growth of homes, programs, and support networks with people who have intellectual disabilities. It was founded in 1964, in France, by Canadian Jean Vanier.

God's Joy

Celebration belongs to God's Kingdom. God not only offers forgiveness, reconciliation, and healing, but wants to lift up these gifts as a source of joy for all who witness them. In all three of the parables that Jesus tells to explain why he eats with sinners, God rejoices and invites others to rejoice with him. "Rejoice with me," the shepherd says, "I have found my sheep that was lost." "Rejoice with me," the woman says, "I have found the drachma I lost." "Rejoice with me," the father says, "this son of mine was lost and is found."

All these voices are the voices of God. God does not want to keep his joy to himself. He wants everyone to share in it. God's joy is the joy of his angels and his saints; it is the joy of all who belong to the Kingdom.

The Return of the Prodigal Son

Joy Flows from Communion with God

The joy that Jesus offers his disciples is his own joy, which flows from his intimate communion with the One who sent him. It is a joy that does not separate happy days from sad days, successful moments from moments of failure, experiences of honor from experiences of dishonor, passion from resurrection. This joy is a divine gift that does not leave us during times of illness, poverty, oppression, or persecution. It is present even when the world laughs or tortures, robs or maims, fights or kills. It is truly ecstatic, always moving us away from the house of fear into the house of love, and always proclaiming that death no longer has the final say, though its noise remains loud and its devastation visible. The joy of Jesus lifts up life to be celebrated.

Lifesigns

In Solitude We Meet Our Loving God

Solitude is the place where *God-with-us* can be unpacked and where we connect with *God-who-is-our-origin,* our loving and benevolent Father and Mother, our Savior, our unconditional Lover. And solitude is the place where our own hearts uncover our deep yearning to be loved unconditionally, and to love with our whole beings. Solitude is indeed the place of the great encounter, from which all other encounters derive their meaning. In solitude we meet the *One-who-calls-us-beloved.* In solitude, we leave behind our many activities, concerns, plans and projects, opinions and convictions to enter into the presence of Love, naked, vulnerable, open, and receptive. Here we encounter a Father/Mother God who is all love, all care, all forgiveness. In solitude we are led to a personal and intimate relationship with Love itself.

Clowning in Rome

Solitude Is the Way to Hope

I ntuitively, we know that it is important to spend time in solitude. We even start looking forward to this strange period
of uselessness. This desire for solitude is often the first sign of
prayer, the first indication that the presence of God's Spirit no
longer remains unnoticed. As we empty ourselves of our many
worries, we come to know not only with our mind but also
with our heart that we never were really alone, that God's Spirit
was with us all along. Thus we come to understand what Paul
writes to the Romans, "Suffering brings patience . . . and patience brings perseverance, and perseverance brings hope, and
this hope is not deceptive, because the love of God has been
poured into our hearts by the Holy Spirit which has been given
to us" (Romans 5:4–5). In solitude, we come to know the Spirit
who has already been given to us. The pains and struggles we
encounter in our solitude thus become the way to hope, because
our hope is not based on something that will happen after our
sufferings are over, but on the real presence of God's healing
Spirit in the midst of these sufferings. The discipline of solitude
allows us gradually to come in touch with this hopeful presence
of God in our lives, and allows us also to taste even now the
beginnings of the joy and peace that belong to the new heaven
and the new earth.

Making All Things New

In Solitude Solidarity

In true solitude there is an unlimited space for others because we are empty. In this poverty nobody stands over and against us, because our enemy is only our enemy as long as we have something to defend. But when we have nothing to hold on to or protect, when we have nothing we consider exclusively ours, then nobody will threaten us. Rather, in the center of our solitude we meet all men and women as brothers and sisters. In true solitude, we stand so naked and so vulnerable before God, and we become so deeply aware of our total dependency on God's love, that not only our friends but also those who kill, lie, torture, rape, and wage wars become part of our flesh and blood. Yes, in true solitude we are so totally empty and poor that we find our solidarity with brothers and sisters everywhere. Our hearts, full of God and empty of fear and anger, become a welcoming home for God and for our whole human family on earth.

Clowning in Rome

We Love Because We Have Been Loved First

Solitude is the ground from which community grows. Whenever we pray alone, study, read, write, or simply spend quiet time away from the places where we interact with each other directly, we are potentially opened for a deeper intimacy with each other. It is a fallacy to think we grow closer to each other only when we talk, play, or work together. Much growth certainly occurs in such human interactions, but these interactions derive their fruit from solitude, because in solitude, our intimacy with each other is deepened. In solitude we discover each other in a way that physical presence makes difficult if not impossible. In solitude we know a bond with each other that does not depend on words, gestures, or actions, a bond much deeper than our own efforts can create. . . .

In solitude we become aware that we were together before we came together and that life is not a creation of our will but rather an obedient response to the reality of our being united. Whenever we enter into solitude, we witness to a love that transcends our interpersonal communications and proclaims that we love each other because we have been loved first (1 John 4:19). Solitude keeps us in touch with the sustaining love from which we draw strength.

Clowning in Rome

You Are the Beloved

Life is a gift. Each one of us is unique, known by name, and loved by the One who fashioned us. Unfortunately, there is a very loud, consistent, and powerful message coming to us from our world that leads us to believe that we must prove our belovedness by how we look, by what we have, and by what we can accomplish. We become preoccupied with "making it" in this life, and we are very slow to grasp the liberating truth of our origins and our finality. We need to hear the message announced and the message emboldened over and over again. Only then do we find the courage to claim it and live from it.

Adam

God's Acceptance of Us
Is Unlimited

O ur true challenge is to return to the center, to the heart, and to find there the gentle voice that speaks to us and affirms us in a way no human voice ever could. The basis of all ministry is the experience of God's unlimited and unlimiting acceptance of us as beloved children, an acceptance so full, so total and all-embracing, that it sets us free from our compulsion to be seen, praised, and admired and frees us for Christ, who leads us on the road of service.

This experience of God's acceptance frees us from our needy self and thus creates new space where we can pay selfless attention to others. This new freedom in Christ allows us to move in the world uninhibited by our compulsions and to act creatively even when we are laughed at and rejected, even when our words and actions lead us to death.

The Selfless Way of Christ

A Converted Heart

Compassion born in solitude makes us very much aware of our own historicity. We are not called to respond to generalities but to the concrete facts with which we are confronted day after day. A compassionate man can no longer look at these manifestations of evil and death as disturbing interruptions of his life plan but rather has to confront them as an opportunity for the conversion of himself and his fellow human beings. Every time in history that men and women have been able to respond to the events of their world as an occasion to change their hearts, an inexhaustible source of generosity and new life has been opened, offering hope far beyond the limits of human prediction.

Reaching Out

Not Me but God

Compassion lies at the heart of our prayer for our fellow human beings. When I pray for the world, I become the world; when I pray for the endless needs of the millions, my soul expands and wants to embrace them all and bring them into the presence of God. But in the midst of that experience I realize that compassion is not mine but God's gift to me. I cannot embrace the world, but God can. I cannot pray, but God can pray in me. When God became as we are, that is, when God allowed all of us to enter into his intimate life, it became possible for us to share in his infinite compassion.

In praying for others, I lose myself and become the other, only to be found by the divine love that holds the whole of humanity in a compassionate embrace.

The Genesee Diary

Compassion Is Being With

L et us not underestimate how hard it is to be compassionate. Compassion is hard because it requires the inner disposition to go with others to the place where they are weak, vulnerable, lonely, and broken. But this is not our spontaneous response to suffering. What we desire most is to do away with suffering by fleeing from it or finding a quick cure for it. As busy, active, relevant [people], we want to earn our bread by making a real contribution. This means first and foremost doing something to show that our presence makes a difference. And so we ignore our greatest gift, which is our ability to enter into solidarity with those who suffer. . . .

Those who can sit with their fellow man, not knowing what to say but knowing that they should be there, can bring new life into a dying heart. Those who are not afraid to hold a hand in gratitude, to shed tears of grief, and to let a sigh of distress arise straight from the heart can break through paralyzing boundaries and witness the birth of a new fellowship, the fellowship of the broken.

The Way of the Heart; Out of Solitude

You Are Part of the Human Family

One of the greatest human spiritual tasks is to embrace all of humanity, to allow your heart to be a marketplace of humanity, to allow your interior life to reflect the pains and the joys of people not only from Africa and Ireland and Yugoslavia and Russia but also from people who lived in the fourteenth century and will live many centuries forward. Somehow, if you discover that your little life is part of the journey of humanity and that you have the privilege to be part of that, your interior life shifts. You lose a lot of fear and something really happens to you. Enormous joy can come into your life. It can give you a strong sense of solidarity with the human race, with the human condition.

It is good to be human.

"Caring for the Whole Person"

Compassionate Solidarity

When we think about the people who have given us hope and have increased the strength of our soul, we might discover that they were not advice givers, warners, or moralists, but the few who were able to articulate in words and actions the human condition in which we participate and who encouraged us to face the realities of life.... Those who do not run away from our pains but touch them with compassion bring healing and new strength. The paradox indeed is that the beginning of healing is in the solidarity with the pain. In our solution-oriented society it is more important than ever to realize that wanting to alleviate pain without sharing it is like wanting to save a child from a burning house without the risk of being hurt. It is in solitude that this compassionate solidarity takes its shape.

Reaching Out

Free to Be Compassionate

If you would ask the Desert Fathers why solitude gives birth to compassion, they would say, "Because it makes us die to our neighbor." At first this answer seems quite disturbing to a modern mind. But when we give it a closer look we can see that in order to be of service to others we have to die to them; that is, we have to give up measuring our meaning and value with the yardstick of others. To die to our neighbors means to stop judging them, to stop evaluating them, and thus to become free to be compassionate. Compassion can never coexist with judgment because judgment creates the distance, the distinction, that prevents us from really being with the other.

The Way of the Heart

Creating the New World to Come

People of prayer are, in the final analysis, people who are able to recognize in others the face of the Messiah. They are people who make visible what was hidden, who make touchable what was unreachable. People of prayer are leaders because precisely through their articulation of God's work within themselves they can lead others away from confusion and toward clarification; through their compassion they can guide others out of the closed circuits of in-groups and toward the wider world of humanity; and through their critical contemplation they can convert convulsive destructiveness into creative work for the new world to come.

The Wounded Healer

Your Suffering Is My Suffering

Compassion means to become close to the one who suffers. But we can come close to another person only when we are willing to become vulnerable ourselves. A compassionate person says: "I am your brother; I am your sister; I am human, fragile, and mortal, just like you. I am not scandalized by your tears, nor afraid of your pain. I, too, have wept. I, too, have felt pain." We can be with the other only when the other ceases to be "other" and becomes like us.

This, perhaps, is the main reason that we sometimes find it easier to show pity than compassion. The suffering person calls us to become aware of our own suffering. How can I respond to someone's loneliness unless I am in touch with my own experience of loneliness? How can I be close to handicapped people when I refuse to acknowledge my own handicaps? How can I be with the poor when I am unwilling to confess my own poverty?

Here and Now

Inviting Closeness with the Other

To care means first of all to empty our own cup and to allow the other to come close to us. It means to take away the many barriers that prevent us from entering into communion with the other. When we dare to care, then we discover that nothing human is foreign to us, but that all the hatred and love, cruelty and compassion, fear and joy can be found in our own hearts. When we dare to care, we have to confess that when others kill, I could have killed, too. When others torture, I could have done the same. When others heal, I could have healed, too. And when others give life, I could have done the same. Then we experience that we can be present to the soldier who kills, to the guard who pesters, to the young man who plays as if life has no end, and to the old man who stopped playing out of fear for death.

By the honest recognition and confession of our human sameness we can participate in the care of God who came, not to the powerful but powerless, not to be different but the same, not to take our pain away but to share it. Through this participation we can open our hearts to each other and form a new community.

Out of Solitude

The Friend Who Cares

When we honestly ask ourselves which persons in our lives mean the most to us, we often find that it is those who, instead of giving much advice, solutions, or cures, have chosen rather to share our pain and touch our wounds with a gentle and tender hand. The friend who can be silent with us in a moment of despair or confusion, who can stay with us in an hour of grief and bereavement, who can tolerate not-knowing, not-curing, not-healing, and face with us the reality of our powerlessness, that is the friend who cares.

Out of Solitude

Cure Without Care

Our tendency is to run away from the painful realities or to try to change them as soon as possible. But cure without care makes us into rulers, controllers, manipulators, and prevents a real community from taking shape. Cure without care makes us preoccupied with quick changes, impatient and unwilling to share each other's burden. And so cure can often become offending instead of liberating.

Out of Solitude

Life Is a Gift to Be Shared

What then is care? The word *care* finds its origin in the word *kara*, which means "to lament, to mourn, to participate in suffering, to share in pain." To care is to cry out with those who are ill, confused, lonely, isolated, and forgotten, and to recognize their pains in our own heart. To care is to enter into the world of those who are only touched by hostile hands, to listen attentively to those whose words are only heard by greedy ears, and to speak gently with those who are used to harsh orders and impatient requests. To care is to be present to those who suffer and to stay present even when nothing can be done to change their situation. To care is to be compassionate and so to form a community of people honestly facing the painful reality of our finite existence. To care is the most human gesture, in which the courageous confession of our common brokenness does not lead to paralysis but to community. When the humble confession of our basic human brokenness forms the ground from which all skillful healing comes forth, then cure can be welcomed not as a property to be claimed, but as a gift to be shared in gratitude.

Care and the Elderly

Acknowledging Our Own Mortality

To care for the elderly means then that we allow the elderly to make us poor by inviting us to give up the illusion that we created our own life and that nothing or nobody can take it away from us. This poverty, which is an inner detachment, can make us free to receive the old stranger into our lives and make that person into a most intimate friend.

When care has made us poor by detaching us from the illusion of immortality, we can really become present to the elderly. We can then listen to what they say without worrying about how we can answer. We can pay attention to what they have to offer without being concerned about what we can give. We can see what they are in themselves without wondering what we can be for them. When we have emptied ourselves of false occupations and preoccupations, we can offer free space to old strangers, where not only bread and wine but also the story of life can be shared.

Aging

Know Yourself

There can hardly be a better image of caring than that of the artist who brings new life to people by his honest and fearless self-portrait. Rembrandt painted his sixty-three self-portraits not just as "a model for studies in expression" but as a "search for the spiritual through the channel of his innermost personality."[*] Rembrandt felt that he had to enter into his own self, into his dark cellars as well as into his light rooms, if he really wanted to penetrate the mystery of man's interiority. Rembrandt realized that what is most personal is most universal. While growing in age he was more and more able to touch the core of the human experience, in which individuals in their misery can recognize themselves and find "courage and new youth." We will never be able to really care if we are not willing to paint and repaint constantly our self-portrait, not as a morbid self-preoccupation, but as a service to those who are searching for some light in the midst of the darkness.

Aging

---

[*] Horst Gerson, *Rembrandt Paintings* (New York: Reynal and Company, 1968), pp. 478 and 460.

Getting Comfortable with Our Own Aging

Caring is first a way to our own aging self, where we can find the healing powers for all those who share in the human condition. No guest will ever feel welcome when the host is not at home in his own house. No old man or woman will ever feel free to reveal his or her hidden anxieties or deeper desires when they only trigger off uneasy feelings in those who are trying to listen. It is no secret that many of our suggestions, advice, admonitions, and good words are often offered in order to keep distance rather than allow closeness. When we are primarily concerned with giving old people something to do, offering them entertainment and distractions, we might avoid the painful realization that most people do not want to be distracted but heard, not entertained but sustained.

Aging

You Are a Recipient of Light

I t is indeed the task of everyone who cares to prevent people—young, middle-aged, and old—from clinging to false expectations and from building their lives on false suppositions. If it is true that people age the way they live, our first task is to help people discover their lifestyles in which "being" is not identified with "having," self-esteem does not depend on success, and goodness is not the same as popularity. Care for the aging means a persistent refusal to attach any kind of ultimate significance to grades, degrees, positions, promotions, or rewards and the courageous effort to keep men and women in contact with their inner self, where they can experience their own solitude and silence as potential recipients of light. When one has not discovered and experienced the light that is love, peace, forgiveness, gentleness, kindness, and deep joy in the early years, how can one expect to recognize it in old age? As the book of Sirach says: "If you have gathered nothing in your youth, how can you find anything in your old age?" (Sirach 25:3–4). That is true not only of money and material goods, but also of peace and purity of heart.

Aging

A Prayer

O Lord, who else or what else can I desire but you? You are my Lord, Lord of my heart, mind, and soul. You know me through and through. In and through you everything that is finds its origin and goal. You embrace all that exists and care for it with divine love and compassion. Why, then, do I keep expecting happiness and satisfaction outside of you? Why do I keep relating to you as one of my many relationships, instead of my only relationship, in which all other ones are grounded? Why do I keep looking for popularity, respect from others, success, acclaim, and sensual pleasures? Why, Lord, is it so hard for me to make you the only one? Why do I keep hesitating to surrender myself totally to you?

Help me, O Lord, to let my old self die, to let me die to the thousand big and small ways in which I am still building up my false self and trying to cling to my false desires. Let me be reborn in you and see through you the world in the right way, so that all my actions, words, and thoughts can become a hymn of praise to you.

I need your loving grace to travel on this hard road that leads to the death of my old self to a new life in and for you. I know and trust that this is the road to freedom.

Lord, dispel my mistrust and help me become a trusting friend.

Amen.

A Cry for Mercy

JULY

Gratitude Is a Quality of the Heart

Gratitude is the awareness that life in all its manifestations is a gift for which we want to give thanks. The closer we come to God in prayer, the more we become aware of the abundance of God's gifts to us. We may even discover the presence of these gifts in the midst of our pains and sorrows. The mystery of the spiritual life is that many of the events, people, and situations that for a long time seemed to inhibit our way to God become ways of being united more deeply with him. What seemed a hindrance proves to be a gift. Thus gratitude becomes a quality of our hearts that allows us to live joyfully and peacefully even though our struggles continue.

A Cry for Mercy

The Choice of Gratitude

Gratitude ... goes beyond the "mine" and "thine" and claims the truth that all of life is a pure gift. In the past I always thought of gratitude as a spontaneous response to the awareness of gifts received, but now I realize that gratitude can also be lived as a discipline. The discipline of gratitude is the explicit effort to acknowledge that all I am and have is given to me as a gift of love, a gift to be celebrated with joy.

Gratitude as a discipline involves a conscious choice. I can choose to be grateful even when my emotions and feelings are still steeped in hurt and resentment. It is amazing how many occasions present themselves in which I can choose gratitude instead of a complaint. . . . The choice for gratitude rarely comes without some real effort. But each time I make it, the next choice is a little easier, a little freer, a little less self-conscious. . . . There is an Estonian proverb that says: "Who does not thank for little will not thank for much." Acts of gratitude make one grateful because, step by step, they reveal that all is grace.

The Return of the Prodigal Son

Everything Is Indeed Good

I just returned from a walk through the dark woods. It was cool and windy, but everything spoke of you. Everything: the clouds, the trees, the wet grass, the valley with its distant lights, the sound of the wind. They all spoke of your resurrection; they all made me aware that everything is indeed good. In you all is created good, and by you all creation is renewed and brought to an even greater glory than it possessed at its beginning.

O Lord, I know now that it is in silence, in a quiet moment, in a forgotten corner that you will meet me, call me by name and speak to me a word of peace. It is in my stillest hour that you become the risen Lord to me.

A Cry for Mercy

The Preciousness of Life

t is not so difficult to understand why, through all the ages, people searching for the meaning of life tried to live as close to nature as possible. Not only St. Benedict, St. Francis, and St. Bruno in the olden days, but also Thomas Merton, who lived in the woods of Kentucky, and the Benedictine monks who built their monastery in an isolated canyon in New Mexico. It is not so strange that many young people are leaving the cities and going out into the country to find peace by listening to the voices of nature. And nature indeed speaks: the birds to St. Francis, the trees to the Native Americans, the river to Siddhartha. And the closer we come to nature, the closer we touch the core of life when we celebrate. Nature makes us aware of the preciousness of life. Nature tells us that life is precious not only because it is, but also because it does not have to be.

Creative Ministry

Nature Is a Gift

In recent decades we have become particularly aware of the crucial importance of our relationship with nature. As long as we relate to the trees, the rivers, the mountains, the fields, and the oceans as properties to be manipulated by us according to our real or fabricated needs, nature remains opaque and does not reveal to us its true being. When we relate to a tree as nothing more than a potential chair, it cannot speak much to us about growth. When a river is only a dumping place for our industrial wastes, it no longer informs us about movement. And when we relate to a flower as nothing more than a model for a plastic decoration, the flower loses its power to reveal to us the simple beauty of life. When we relate to nature primarily as property to be used, it becomes opaque, and this opaqueness is manifested in our society as pollution. The dirty rivers, the smog-filled skies, the strip-mined hills, and the ravaged woods are sad signs of our false relationship with nature.

Our difficult and very urgent task is to accept the truth that nature is not primarily a property to be possessed, but a gift to be received with admiration and gratitude. Only when we make a deep bow to the rivers, oceans, hills, and mountains that offer us a home, only then can they become transparent and reveal to us their real meaning.

Clowning in Rome

Nature Points to God's Love

All nature conceals its great secrets and cannot reveal its hidden wisdom and profound beauty if we do not listen carefully and patiently. John Henry Newman sees nature as a veil through which an invisible world is intimated. He writes:

"The visible world is . . . the veil of the world invisible . . . so that all that exists or happens visibly, conceals and yet suggests, and above all subserves, a system of persons, facts, and events beyond itself."*

How differently we would live if we were constantly aware of this veil and sensed in our whole being how nature is ever ready for us to hear and see the great story of the Creator's love, to which it points. The plants and animals with whom we live teach us about birth, growth, maturation, and death, about the need for gentle care, and especially about the importance of patience and hope. . . .

It is sad that in our days we are less connected with nature and we no longer allow nature to minister to us. We so easily limit ministry to work for people by people. But we could do an immense service to our world if we would let nature heal, counsel, and teach again. I often wonder if the sheer artificiality and ugliness with which many people are surrounded are not as bad as or worse than their interpersonal problems.

Clowning in Rome

---

* John Henry Newman, *Essays Critical and Historical,* vol. 2 (London: Longmans, Green and Co., 1901), p. 192.

God Loves Us from Eternity to Eternity

have always been very conscious of my clock-time. Often I asked myself: "Can I still double my years?" When I was thirty I said: "I can easily live another thirty!" When I was forty, I mused, "Maybe I am only halfway!" Today I can no longer say that, and my question has become: "How am I going to use the few years left to me?" All these concerns about our clock-time come from below. They are based on the presupposition that our chronology is all we have to live. But looked upon from above, from God's perspective, our clock-time is embedded in the timeless embrace of God. Looked upon from above, our years on earth are not simply *chronos*, but *kairos*—another Greek word for time—which is the opportunity to claim for ourselves the love that God offers us from eternity to eternity.

Here and Now

What We're Looking for Is Already Here

To start seeing that the many events of our day, week, or year are not in the way of our search for a full life but are rather the way to it is a real experience of conversion. We discover that cleaning and cooking, writing letters and doing professional work, visiting people and caring for others, are not a series of random events that prevent us from realizing our deepest self. These natural, daily activities contain within them some transforming power that changes how we live. We make hidden passage from time lived as *chronos* to time lived as *kairos*. *Kairos* is a Greek word meaning "the opportunity." It is the right time, the real moment, the chance of our lives. When our time becomes *kairos,* it frees us and opens us to endless new possibilities. Living *kairos* offers us an opportunity for a profound change of heart.

Clowning in Rome

The Eternal in the Present

All the events of life, even such dark events as war, famine and flood, violence and murder, are not irreversible fatalities. Each moment is like a seed that carries within itself the possibility of becoming *the* moment of change. . . . We no longer need to run from present time in search of the place where we think life is really happening. We begin to have a truer vision of the world and of our lives in relationship to time and eternity. We begin to glimpse something of eternity in time. At this point boredom falls away and the joyful and painful moments of our lives take on new and profound meaning. It is then that we know that for us time is becoming transparent.

The contemplative life, therefore, is not a life that offers a few good moments between the many bad ones, but a life that transforms all our time into a window through which the invisible world becomes visible.

Clowning in Rome

It's All How You Look at It

The great conversion in our life is to recognize and believe that the many unexpected events are not just disturbing interruptions in our projects, but the way in which God molds our hearts and prepares us for his return. Our great temptations are boredom and bitterness. When our good plans are interrupted by poor weather, our well-organized careers by illness or bad luck, our peace of mind by inner turmoil, our hope for peace by a new war, our desire for a stable government by a constant changing of the guards, and our desire for immortality by real death, we are tempted to give in to a paralyzing boredom or to strike back in destructive bitterness. But when we believe that patience can make our expectations grow, then fate can be converted into a vocation, wounds into a call for deeper understanding, and sadness into a birthplace of joy.

Out of Solitude

The Most Universal Is the Most Personal

When only our minds and hands work together we quickly become dependent on the results of our actions and tend to give up when they do not materialize. In the solitude of the heart we can truly listen to the pains of the world because there we can recognize them not as strange and unfamiliar pains, but as pains that are indeed our own. There we can see that what is most universal is most personal and that indeed nothing human is strange to us. There we can feel that the cruel reality of history is indeed the reality of the human heart, our own included, and that to protest asks, first of all, for a confession of our own participation in the human condition. There we can indeed respond.

Reaching Out

July

12

The Way of Change

I t is my growing conviction that in Jesus the mystical and the revolutionary ways are not opposites, but two sides of the same human mode of experiential transcendence. I am increasingly convinced that conversion is the individual equivalent of revolution. Therefore, every real revolutionary is challenged to be a mystic at heart, and one who walks the mystical way is called to unmask the illusory quality of human society.

Mysticism and revolution are two aspects of the same attempt to bring about radical change. Mystics cannot prevent themselves from becoming social critics, since in self-reflection they will discover the roots of a sick society. Similarly, revolutionaries cannot avoid facing their own human condition, since in the midst of their struggle for a new world they will find that they are also fighting their own reactionary fears and false ambitions.

The Wounded Healer

Creative Reciprocity

We who want to bring about change have first of all to learn to be changed by those whom we want to help. This, of course, is exceptionally difficult for those who are undergoing their first exposure to an area of distress. They see poor houses, hungry people, dirty streets; they hear people cry in pain without medical care, they smell unwashed bodies, and in general are overwhelmed by the misery that is all around them. But none of us will be able to really give if he has not discovered that what he gives is only a small thing compared to what we have received. When Jesus says: "Happy the poor, the hungry, and the weeping" (Luke 6:21), we have to be able to *see* that happiness. When Jesus says: "What you did to the least of my brothers, you did to me" (Matthew 25:40), he is addressing to us a direct invitation not only to help but also to discover the beauty of God in those who are to be helped. As long as we see only distasteful poverty, we are not really entitled to give. When, however, we find people who have truly devoted themselves to work in the slums and the ghettos and who feel that their vocation is to be of service there, we find that they have discovered that in the smiles of the children, the hospitality of the people; the expressions they use, the stories they tell, the wisdom they show, the goods they share; there is hidden so much richness and beauty, so much affection and human warmth, that the work they are doing is only a small return for what they have already received.

Creative Ministry

Re-Creating God's Presence

All Christian action—whether it is visiting the sick, feeding the hungry, clothing the naked, or working for a more just and peaceful society—is a manifestation of the human solidarity revealed to us in the house of God. It is not an anxious human effort to create a better world. It is a confident expression of the truth that in Christ, death, evil, and destruction have been overcome. It is not a fearful attempt to restore a broken order. It is a joyful assertion that in Christ all order has already been restored. It is not a nervous effort to bring divided people together, but a celebration of an already established unity. This action is not activism. An activist wants to heal, restore, redeem, and re-create, but those acting within the house of God point through their action to the healing, restoring, redeeming, and re-creating presence of God.

Lifesigns

You Do Not Belong to the World

I think for peacemaking it is so important that we are home, that we know to whom we belong. Jesus says it very clearly; he says: "You do not belong to the world, just as I do not belong to the world. Therefore, I am sending you into the world as my Father has sent me into the world." You have to catch the paradox: that we can really be in the world, involved in the world, and actively engaged in the world precisely because we do not belong to it, precisely because that is not where our dwelling place is. Precisely because our home is in God, we can be in the world, and speak words of healing, of confrontation, of invitation, and of challenge.

"Spirituality, Peacemaking, and the Gospel of John"

The Divine Choice of Weakness

God chose to enter into human history in complete weakness. That divine choice forms the center of the Christian faith. In Jesus of Nazareth, the powerless God appeared among us to unmask the illusion of power, to disarm the prince of darkness who rules the world, and to bring the divided human race to a new unity. It is through total and unmitigated powerlessness that God shows us divine mercy. . . . It is very hard—if not impossible—for us to grasp this divine mercy. We keep praying to the "almighty and powerful God." But all might and power is absent from the One who reveals God to us saying: "When you see me, you see the Father." If we truly want to love God, we have to look at the man of Nazareth, whose life was wrapped in weakness. And his weakness opens for us the way to the heart of God.

Finding My Way Home

God Is Perfect Love

Often we use the word *God*. This word can suggest something fascinating as well as horrible, attractive as well as repelling, seductive as well as dangerous, all-absorbing as well as nourishing. It is like the sun. Without the sun, there can be no life, but if we come too close to it, we are burned. The Christian, however, believes that God is no "something," but rather a person who is Love—perfect Love. The Christian knows it is possible to enter into dialogue with this loving God and so work at renewing the earth. Praying, therefore, is the most critical activity we are capable of, for when we pray, we are never satisfied with the world of the here and now and are constantly striving to realize the new world, the first glimmers of which we have already seen.

With Open Hands

God Doesn't Get Burned Out

Exhaustion, burnout, and depression are not signs that you are doing God's will. God is gentle and loving. God desires to give you a deep sense of safety in God's love. Once you have allowed yourself to experience that love fully, you will be better able to discern who you are being sent to in God's name.

The Inner Voice of Love

Bring All Your Thoughts to God

Although many good things have been written about contemplation and contemplative prayer, many people still have the impression that contemplative prayer is something very special, very "high," or very difficult, and really not for ordinary people with ordinary jobs and ordinary problems. This is unfortunate because the discipline of contemplative prayer is particularly valuable for those who have so much on their minds that they suffer from fragmentation. If it is true that all Christians are called to bring their thoughts into an ongoing conversation with their Lord, then contemplative prayer can be a discipline that is especially important for those who are deeply involved in the many affairs of the world.

Clowning in Rome

God's Heart Has Become One with Ours

When we say to people, "I will pray for you," we make a very important commitment. The sad thing is that this remark often remains nothing but a well-meant expression of concern. But when we learn to descend with our mind into our heart, then all those who have become part of our lives are led into the healing presence of God and touched by him in the center of our being. We are speaking here about a mystery for which words are inadequate. It is the mystery that the heart, which is the center of our being, is transformed by God into his own heart, a heart large enough to embrace the entire universe. Through prayer we can carry in our heart all human pain and sorrow, all conflicts and agonies, all torture and war, all hunger, loneliness, and misery, not because of some great psychological or emotional capacity, but because God's heart has become one with ours.

The Way of the Heart

Proclaiming God's Love

I t seems the closer I come to the poor and broken people of the world, the greater my desire is to speak directly about God and the less I feel impelled to deal with the burning issues of our day. This doesn't mean that I am not any more interested in these issues; in fact, I am more interested in them than ever, but somehow the way I enter into these issues has shifted. Presently, I am very much involved in the life of handicapped people and I am becoming more and more involved in the struggles of people who have AIDS as well as people who live with great inner anguish and pain. Somehow these people are calling me to be more and more God-centered and seem to ask me less to help them solve their problems than to reveal to them God's immense and intimate love for them.

Love, Henri

We Are a People of Hope

The state of the world suggests to me the urgent need for a spirituality that takes the end things very seriously, not a spirituality of withdrawal, nor of blindness to the powers of the world, but a spirituality that allows us to live in this world without belonging to it, a spirituality that allows us to take the joy and peace of the divine life even when we are surrounded by the powers and principalities of evil, death, and destruction. I wonder if a spirituality of liberation does not need to be deepened by a spirituality of exile or captivity. I wonder if a spirituality that focuses on the alleviation of poverty should not be deepened by a spirituality that allows people to continue their lives when their poverty only increases. I wonder if a spirituality that encourages peacemaking should not be deepened by a spirituality that allows us to remain faithful when the only things we see are dying children, burning houses, and the total destruction of our civilization. May God prevent any of these horrors from taking place, may we do all that is possible to prevent them, but may we never lose our faith when "great misery [descends] on the land and wrath on this people . . . [when there are] signs in the sun and moon and stars . . . [when] nations [are] in agony, bewildered by the clamor of the ocean and its waves" (Luke 21:24–26). I pray that we will not be swept away by our own curiosity, sensationalism, and panic, but remain attentive to him who comes and will say: "Come, you whom my Father has blessed, take for your heritage the kingdom prepared for you since the foundation of the world" (Matthew 25:34–35).

Gracias!

God Stays with Us

I really don't know if our civilization will survive the century. Considering the growing threat of nuclear holocaust there certainly is a reason to wonder. But important for me is not if our civilization will survive or not but if we can continue to live with hope, and I really think we can because our Lord has given us his promise that he will stay with us at all times. He is the God of the living. He has overcome evil and death and his love is stronger than any form of death and destruction. That is why I feel that we should continually avoid the temptation of despair and deepen our awareness that God is present in the midst of all the chaos that surrounds us and that that presence allows us to live joyfully and peacefully in a world so filled with sorrow and conflict.

Love, Henri

Love God with All Your Heart

Jesus' primary concern was to be obedient to his Father, to live constantly in his presence. Only then did it become clear to him what his task was in his relationships with people. This also is the way he proposes for his apostles: "It is to the glory of my Father that you should bear much fruit, and then you will be my disciples" (John 15:8). Perhaps we must continually remind ourselves that the first commandment requiring us to love God with all our heart, all our soul, and all our mind is indeed the first. I wonder if we really believe this. It seems that in fact we live as if we should give as much of our heart, soul, and mind as possible to our fellow human beings, while trying hard not to forget God. At least we feel that our attention should be divided evenly between God and our neighbor. But Jesus' claim is much more radical. He asks for a single-minded commitment to God and God alone. God wants all of our heart, all of our mind, and all of our soul. It is this unconditional and unreserved love for God that leads to the care for our neighbor, not as an activity that distracts us from God or competes with our attention to God, but as an expression of our love for God who reveals himself to us as the God of all people. It is in God that we find our neighbors and discover our responsibility to them. We might even say that only in God does our neighbor become a neighbor rather than an infringement upon our autonomy, and that only in and through God does service become possible.

The Living Reminder

In Service We Encounter God

Radical servanthood does not make sense unless we introduce a new level of understanding and see it as the way to encounter God. To be humble and persecuted cannot be desired unless we can find God in humility and persecution. When we begin to see God, the source of all our comfort and consolation, in the center of servanthood, compassion becomes much more than doing good for unfortunate people. Radical servanthood, as the encounter with the compassionate God, takes us beyond the distinctions between wealth and poverty, success and failure, fortune and bad luck. Radical servanthood is not an enterprise in which we try to surround ourselves with as much misery as possible, but a joyful way of life in which our eyes are opened to the vision of the true God who chose to be revealed in servanthood. The poor are called blessed not because poverty is good, but because theirs is the kingdom of heaven; the mourners are called blessed not because mourning is good, but because they shall be comforted.

Here we are touching the profound spiritual truth that service is an expression of the search for God and not just of the desire to bring about individual or social change.

Compassion

Letting Go of Fear

Underneath all our emphasis on successful action, many of us suffer from a deep-seated, low self-esteem. . . . And so our actions become more an expression of fear than of inner freedom. . . .

As we keep our eyes directed at the One who says, "Do not be afraid," we may slowly let go of our fear. We will learn to live in a world without zealously defended borders. We will be free to see the suffering of other people, free to respond not with defensiveness, but with compassion, with peace, with ourselves.

Out of Solitude; Turn My Mourning into Dancing

Sharing Our Weakness

O ver the last few years I have been increasingly aware that true healing mostly takes place through the sharing of weakness. Mostly we are so afraid of our weaknesses that we hide them at all cost and thus make them unavailable to others but also often to ourselves. And, in this way, we end up living double lives even against our own desires: one life in which we present ourselves to the world, to ourselves, and to God as a person who is in control and another life in which we feel insecure, doubtful, confused, and anxious and totally out of control. The split between these two lives causes us a lot of suffering. I have become increasingly aware of the importance of overcoming the great chasm between these two lives and am becoming more and more aware that facing, with others, the reality of our existence can be the beginning of a truly free life.

It is amazing in my own life that true friendship and community became possible to the degree that I was able to share my weaknesses with others. Often I became aware of the fact that in the sharing of my weaknesses with others, the real depths of my human brokenness and weakness and sinfulness started to reveal themselves to me, not as a source of despair but as a source of hope. As long as I try to convince myself or others of my independence, a lot of my energy is invested in building up my own false self. But once I am able to truly confess my most profound dependence on others and on God, I can come in touch with my true self and real community can develop.

Love, Henri

The Divine Gift of Unity

Jesus prays for unity among his disciples and among those who through the teaching of his disciples will come to believe in him. He says: "May they all be one, just as, Father, you are in me and I in you . . ." (John 17:21).

These words of Jesus reveal the mystery that unity among people is not first of all the result of human effort, but rather a divine gift. Unity among people is a reflection of the unity of God. The desire for unity is deep and strong among people. It is a desire between friends, between married people, between communities, and between countries. Wherever there is a true experience of unity, there is a sense of giftedness. While unity satisfies our deepest need, it cannot be explained by what we say or do. There exists no formula for unity.

When Jesus prays for unity, he asks his Father that those who believe in him, that is, in his full communion with the Father, will become part of that unity. I continue to see in myself and others how often we try to make unity among ourselves by focusing all our attention on each other and trying to find the place where we can feel united. But often we become disillusioned, realizing that no human being is capable of offering us what we most want. Such disillusionment can easily make us become bitter, cynical, demanding, even violent.

Jesus calls us to seek our unity in and through him. When we direct our inner attention not first of all to each other, but to God to whom we belong, then we will discover that in God we also belong to each other.

The Road to Daybreak

Can We Recognize His Presence?

The world in which we live today and about whose suffering we know so much seems more than ever a world from which Christ has withdrawn himself. How can I believe that in this world we are constantly being prepared to receive the Spirit? Still, I think that this is exactly the message of hope. God has not withdrawn himself. He sent his Son to share our human condition and the Son sent us his Spirit to lead us into the intimacy of his divine life. It is in the midst of the chaotic suffering of humanity that the Holy Spirit, the Spirit of Love, makes himself visible. But can we recognize his presence?

The Genesee Diary

Claim Your Peace

really wish you an ever deeper peace. I know that that peace quite often lives underneath the turmoils and anxieties of our heart and doesn't always mean inner harmony or emotional tranquility. That peace that God gives us quite often is beyond our thoughts and feelings, and we have to really trust that peace is there for us to claim even in the midst of our moments of despair.

Love, Henri

A Prayer

Dear God,

As you draw me ever deeper into your heart,
I discover that my companions on the
journey are women and men
loved by you as fully and as intimately as I am.
In your compassionate heart,
there is a place for all of them.
No one is excluded.
Give me a share in your compassion, dear God,
so that your unlimited love may become visible
in the way I love my brothers and sisters.

Amen.

With Open Hands

AUGUST

The Sacred and the Holy

S omething very deep and mysterious, very holy and sacred, is taking place in our lives right where we are, and the more attentive we become the more we will begin to see and hear it. The more our spiritual sensitivities come to the surface of our daily lives, the more we will discover—uncover—a new presence in our lives.

A Letter of Consolation

Your Inner Hermitage

Try to keep a little hermitage in the center of your being, where you can continue your prayer even during a busy day.

A simple prayer such as "Lord Jesus Christ, Son of the living God, have mercy on me a sinner" can give you much consolation and strength when you allow it to remain present in your inner hermitage.

It is the way to let the Spirit of God pray in you.

Unpublished letter

Let God Love You the Way God Wants

know that true joy comes from letting God love me the way God wants, whether it is through illness or health, failure or success, poverty or wealth, rejection or praise. It is hard for me to say, "I shall gratefully accept everything, Lord, that pleases you. Let your will be done." But I know that when I truly believe my Father is pure love, it will become increasingly possible to say these words from the heart.

Charles de Foucauld once wrote a prayer of abandonment that expresses beautifully the spiritual attitude I wish I had.

Father, I abandon myself into your hands,
do with me what you will.
Whatever you may do, I thank you;
I am ready for all, I accept all.
Let only your will be done in me, and in all your creatures.

I wish no more than this, O Lord.

Into your hands I commend my soul;
I offer it to you with all the love of my heart,
for I love you, Lord, and so need to give myself,
to surrender myself into your hands without reserve,
and with boundless confidence, for you are my Father.

It seems good to pray this prayer often. These are words of a holy man, and they show the way I must go. I realize that I can never make this prayer come true by my own efforts. But the Spirit of Jesus given to me can help me pray it and grow to its fulfillment. I know that my inner peace depends on my willingness to make this prayer my own.

The Road to Daybreak

Where to Put Our Attention

S omewhere we know that without silence words lose their meaning, that without listening speaking no longer heals, that without distance closeness cannot cure. Somewhere we know that without a lonely place our actions quickly become empty gestures. The careful balance between silence and words, withdrawal and involvement, distance and closeness, solitude and community forms the basis of the Christian life and should, therefore, be the subject of our most personal attention.

Out of Solitude

Know What the Scoop Is

The contemplative is someone who sees things for what they really are, who sees the real connections, who knows—as Thomas Merton used to say—"what the scoop is." To attain such a vision, a spiritual discipline is necessary. Evagrius [Ponticus] calls discipline the *praktike*, removing the blindfolds that prevent us from seeing clearly. Merton, himself very familiar with Evagrius, expressed the same idea. He told the monks of Gethsemani Abbey that the contemplative life is a life in which we constantly move from opaqueness to transparency, from the place where things are dark, impenetrable, and closed to the place where these same things are translucent, open, and offer vision far beyond themselves.

Clowning in Rome

Being Is More Important Than Doing

suspect that we too often have lost contact with the source of our own existence and have become strangers in our own house. We tend to run around trying to solve the problems of our world while anxiously avoiding confrontation with that reality wherein our problems find their deepest roots: our own selves. In many ways we are like the busy executive who walks up to a precious flower and says: "What for God's sake are you doing here? Can't you get busy somehow?" and then finds the flower's response incomprehensible: "I am sorry, but I am just here to be beautiful."

How can we also come to this wisdom of the flower that being is more important than doing? How can we come to a creative contact with the grounding of our own life?

Creative Ministry

We Are Called to Be Fruitful

You have to be really aware of the difference between fruitfulness and success because the world is always talking to you about your success. Society keeps asking you: "Show me your trophies. Show me, how many books have you written? Show me, how many games did you win? Show me, how much money did you make? Show me. . . ." And there is nothing wrong with any of that. I am saying that finally that's not the question. The question is: "Are you going to bear fruit?" And the amazing thing is that our fruitfulness comes out of our vulnerability and not just out of our power. Actually it comes out of our powerlessness. If the ground wants to be fruitful, you have to break it open a little bit. The hard ground cannot bear fruit; it has to be raked open. And the mystery is that our illness and our weakness and our many ways of dying are often the ways that we get in touch with our vulnerabilities. You and I have to trust that they will allow us to be more fruitful if lived faithfully. Precisely where we are weakest and often most broken and most needy, precisely there can be the ground of our fruitfulness. That is the vision that means that death can indeed be the final healing—because it becomes the way to be so vulnerable that we can bear fruit in a whole new way. Like trees that die and become fuel, and like leaves that die and become fertilizer, in nature something new comes out from death all the time. So you have to realize that you are part of that beautiful process, that your death is not the end but in fact it is the source of your fruitfulness beyond you in new generations, in new centuries.

"Caring for the Whole Person"

Witnesses to the Light

S olitude molds self-righteous people into gentle, caring, for-giving persons who are so deeply convinced of their own great sinfulness and so fully aware of God's even greater mercy that their life itself becomes ministry. In such a ministry there is hardly any difference left between doing and being. When we are filled with God's merciful presence, we can do nothing other than minister because our whole being witnesses to the light that has come into the darkness.

The Way of the Heart

Sowing Love

You know something about brokenness. You know about the broken world. You know about brokenness in your country. But most personally, you know it in your more intimate life. You know we are broken people and we suffer very intimate pains. The pain of a desire for intimacy that hasn't been fulfilled . . . the pain of a relationship that did not work . . . the pain of an addiction that is so hard to confess . . . The secret pain of loneliness that can bite us so much . . . And what I would like to say to you is don't be afraid of your pain, but dare to embrace it. If you are wounded, and I know that you and I are, put your brokenness under the blessing.

We are called to give our lives to others, so you and I can bear fruit. And all brokenness, and all dying, and all suffering is there to allow you to enter into solidarity with the whole human family, and to give yourselves to others so that your life can bear fruit. God asks you not to have a successful life but to have a fruitful life.

"Belovedness"

Compassion

Compassion asks us to go where it hurts, to enter into the places of pain, to share in brokenness, fear, confusion, and anguish. Compassion challenges us to cry out with those in misery, to mourn with those who are lonely, to weep with those in tears. Compassion requires us to be weak with the weak, vulnerable with the vulnerable, and powerless with the powerless. Compassion means full immersion in the condition of being human.

Compassion

Nothing Human Is Alien

Through compassion it is possible to recognize that the craving for love that people feel resides also in our own hearts, that the cruelty that the world knows all too well is also rooted in our own impulses. Through compassion we also sense our hope for forgiveness in our friends' eyes and our hatred in their bitter mouths. When they kill, we know that we could have done it; when they give life, we know that we can do the same. For a compassionate man nothing human is alien; no joy and no sorrow, no way of living and no way of dying.

The Wounded Healer

We Are Seen by God's Loving Eyes

The greatest spiritual battle begins—and never ends—with the reclaiming of our chosenness. Long before any human being saw us, we are seen by God's loving eyes. Long before anyone heard us cry or laugh, we are heard by our God who is all ears for us. Long before any person spoke to us in this world, we are spoken to by the voice of eternal love.

Life of the Beloved

The Chosenness of the Other

When we claim and constantly reclaim the truth of being the chosen ones, we soon discover within ourselves a deep desire to reveal to others their own chosenness. Instead of making us feel that we are better, more precious or valuable than others, our awareness of being chosen opens our eyes to the chosenness of others. That is the great joy of being chosen: the discovery that others are chosen as well. In the house of God there are many mansions. There is a place for everyone—a unique, special place. Once we deeply trust that we ourselves are precious in God's eyes, we are able to recognize the preciousness of others and their unique place in God's heart.

Life of the Beloved

Reaching Out

When we have found our own uniqueness in the love of God and have been able to affirm that indeed we are lovable since it is God's love that dwells in us, then we can reach out to others in whom we discover a new and unique manifestation of the same love and enter into an intimate communion with them.

The Genesee Diary

We're on a Pilgrimage

Detachment is often understood as letting loose of what is attractive. But it sometimes also requires letting go of what is repulsive. You can indeed become attached to dark forces such as resentment and hatred. As long as you seek retaliation, you cling to your own past. Sometimes it seems as though you might lose yourself along with your revenge and hate—so you stand there with balled-up fists, closed to the other who wants to heal you. . . .

Praying means, above all, to be accepting of God who is always new, always different. For God is a deeply moved God, whose heart is greater than our own. The open acceptance of prayer in the face of an ever-new God makes us free. In prayer, we are constantly on our way, on a pilgrimage. On our way, we meet more and more people who show us something about the God whom we seek. We will never know for sure if we have reached God. But we do know that God will always be new and that there is no reason to fear.

With Open Hands

Let Go

The world is only evil when you become its slave. The world has a lot to offer—just as Egypt did for the children of Jacob—as long as you don't feel bound to obey it. The great struggle facing you is not to leave the world, to reject your ambitions and aspirations, or to despise money, prestige, or success, but to claim your spiritual truth and to live in the world as someone who doesn't belong to it. . . . All the good things our world has to offer are yours to enjoy. But you can enjoy them truly only when you can acknowledge them as affirmations of the truth that you are the Beloved of God. The truth will set you free to receive the beauty of nature and culture in gratitude, as a sign of your Belovedness. That truth will allow you to receive the gifts you receive from your society and celebrate life. But that truth will also allow you to let go of what distracts you, confuses you, and puts in jeopardy the life of the Spirit within you.

Life of the Beloved

Our Gifts Are Not the Same as Our Talents

More important than our talents are our gifts. We may have only a few talents, but we have many gifts. Our gifts are the many ways in which we express our humanity. They are part of who we are: friendship, kindness, patience, joy, peace, forgiveness, gentleness, love, hope, trust, and many others. These are the true gifts we have to offer to each other.

Somehow I have known this for a long time, especially through my personal experience of the enormous healing power of these gifts. But since my coming to live in a community with mentally handicapped people, I have rediscovered this simple truth. Few, if any, of those people have talents they can boast of. Few are able to make contributions to our society that allow them to earn money, compete on the open market, or win awards. But how splendid are their gifts!

Life of the Beloved

Receiving the Gifts of Others

A gift only becomes a gift when it is received; and nothing we have to give—wealth, talents, competence, or just beauty—will ever be recognized as true gifts until someone is open to accept them. This all suggests that if we want others to grow—that is, to discover their potential and capacities, to experience that they have something to live and work for—we should first of all be able to recognize their gifts and be willing to receive them. For we only become fully human when we are received and accepted.

Creative Ministry

Poverty Is a Quality of the Heart

Poverty is the quality of the heart that makes us relate to life, not as a property to be defended but as a gift to be shared. Poverty is the constant willingness to say good-bye to yesterday and move forward to new, unknown experiences. Poverty is the inner understanding that the hours, days, weeks, and years do not belong to us but are the gentle reminders of our call to give, not only love and work, but life itself, to those who follow us and will take our place. He or she who cares is invited to be poor, to strip himself or herself from the illusions of ownership, and to create some room for the person looking for a place to rest. The paradox of care is that poverty makes a good host. When our hands, heads, and hearts are filled with worries, concerns, and preoccupations, there can hardly be any place left for the stranger to feel at home.

Aging

To Pray Is to Live

Maybe someone will say to you, "You have to forgive yourself." But that isn't possible. What is possible is to open your hands without fear, so that the One who loves you can blow your sins away. Then the coins you considered indispensable for your life prove to be little more than light dust that a soft breeze will whirl away, leaving only a grin or a chuckle behind. Then you feel a bit of new freedom and praying becomes a joy, a spontaneous reaction to the world and the people around you. Praying then becomes effortless, inspired, and lively, or peaceful and quiet. When you recognize the festive and the still moments as moments of prayer, then you gradually realize that to pray is to live.

With Open Hands

We Pray in the Context of Grace

We enter into solitude first of all to meet our Lord and to be with him and him alone. Our primary task in solitude, therefore, is not to pay undue attention to the many faces that assail us, but to keep the eyes of our mind and heart on him who is our divine savior. Only in the context of grace can we face our sin; only in the place of healing do we dare to show our wounds; only with a single-minded attention to Christ can we give up our clinging fears and face our own true nature. As we come to realize that it is not we who live, but Christ who lives in us, that he is our true self, we can slowly let our compulsions melt away and begin to experience the freedom of the children of God. And then we can look back with a smile and realize that we aren't even angry or greedy anymore.

The Way of the Heart

Spiritual Freedom

Freedom belongs to the core of the spiritual life; not just the freedom that releases us from forces that want to oppress us, but the freedom also to forgive others, to serve them, and to form a new bond of fellowship with them. In short, the freedom to love and to work for a free world.

Letters to Marc About Jesus

Offer God Your Imperfections

It is through our broken, vulnerable, mortal ways of being that the healing power of the eternal God becomes visible to us.

We are called each day to present to the Lord the whole of our lives—our joys as well as sorrows, our successes as well as failures, our hopes as well as fears. We are called to do so with our limited means, our stuttering words and halting expressions. In this way we will come to know in mind and heart the unceasing prayer of God's Spirit in us. Our many prayers are in fact confessions of our inability to pray. But they are confessions that enable us to perceive the merciful presence of God.

A Cry for Mercy

Choose a Contained Life

I know how great a temptation it is in times of anguish and agony to look away from our painful center and expect peace and a sense of inner wholeness to come from some external source. But I am increasingly convinced that, at times of anguish and agony, we have to choose a contained life where we can be in the presence of people who hold us safe and bring us in touch with the unconditional affective love of God. Do not get involved in experiences of living that will lead to dissipation. What is so important is to have a deep sense of inner safety, of being held by a love that is in no way using you, manipulating you, or "needing" you.

Unpublished letter

Writing Reveals What Is Alive in Us

Writing is a process in which we discover what lives in us. The writing itself reveals to us what is alive in us. The deepest satisfaction of writing is precisely that it opens up new spaces within us of which we were not aware before we started to write. To write is to embark on a journey whose final destination we do not know. Thus, writing requires a real act of trust. We have to say to ourselves: "I do not yet know what I carry in my heart, but I trust that it will emerge as I write." Writing is like giving away the few loaves and fishes one has, trusting that they will multiply in the giving. Once we dare to "give away" on paper the few thoughts that come to us, we start discovering how much is hidden underneath these thoughts and gradually come in touch with our own riches.

Seeds of Hope

The Beauty of Letter Writing

As I was writing letters today, I realized that writing letters is a much more intimate way of communicating than making phone calls. It may sound strange, but I often feel closer to friends I write than to friends I speak with by phone.

When I write I think deeply about my friends, I pray for them, I tell them my emotions and feelings. I reflect on our relationship, and I dwell with them in a very personal way. Over the past few months I have come to enjoy letter writing more and more. In the beginning it seemed like a heavy burden, but now it is a relaxing time of the day. It feels like interrupting work for a conversation with a friend.

The beauty of letter writing is that it deepens friendships and makes them more real. I have also discovered that letter writing makes me pray more concretely for my friends. Early in the morning I spend a little time praying for each person to whom I have written and promised my prayers.

Today I feel surrounded by the friends I am writing to and praying for. Our love for each other is very concrete and life giving. Thank God for letters, for those who send them, and for those who receive them.

The Road to Daybreak

Live Without Division Between Word and Action

In Jesus, no division existed between his words and his actions, between what he said and what he did. Jesus' words were his action, his words were events. They not only spoke about changes, cures, new life, but they actually created them. In this sense, Jesus is truly the Word made flesh; in that Word all is created and by that Word all is re-created.

Saintliness means living without division between word and action. If I would truly live in my own life the word I am speaking, my spoken words would become actions, and miracles would happen whenever I open my mouth.

Gracias!

From Compromise to Repentance

Knowing Jesus, reading his words, and praying create an increasing clarity about evil and good, sin and grace, Satan and God. This clarity calls me to choose the way to the light fearlessly and straightforwardly. The more I come to know Jesus, the more I also realize how many such choices have to be made and how often. They involve so much more than my public acts. They touch the deepest recesses of the heart, where my most private thoughts and fantasies are hidden.

Reflecting on my life, I saw how opaque it has been. I often did one thing while saying another, said one thing while thinking another, thought one thing while feeling another. I found many examples in which I had even lied to myself. . . .

How to go from this opaqueness to transparency? A transparent life is a life without moral ambiguities in which heart, mind, and gut are united in choosing for the light. I am discovering the importance of naming the darkness in me. By no longer calling the darkness anything else but darkness, the temptation to keep using it for my own selfish purposes gradually becomes less. . . .

A hard task is given to me—to call the darkness darkness, evil evil, and the demon demon. By remaining vague I can avoid commitment and drift along in the mainstream of our society. But Jesus does not allow me to stay there. He requires a clear choice for truth, light, and life. When I recognize my countless inner compromises, I may feel guilty and ashamed at first. But when this leads to repentance and a contrite heart, I will soon discover the immense love of God, who came to lead me out of the darkness into the light and who wants to make me into a transparent witness of his love.

No Hiding

Why do we keep hiding our deepest feelings from each other? We suffer much, but we also have great gifts of healing for each other. The mystery is that by hiding our pain we also hide our ability to heal.... We are called to confess to each other and forgive each other, and thus to discover the abundant mercy of God. But at the same time, we are so terribly afraid of being hurt more than we already are. This fear keeps us prisoners, even when the prison has no walls! I see better every day how radical Jesus' message of love really is.

The Road to Daybreak

Forgiveness

Forgiveness is the name of love practiced among people who love poorly. The hard truth is that all people love poorly. We need to forgive and be forgiven every day, every hour increasingly. That is the great work of love among the fellowship of the weak that is the human family.

"Forgiveness"

A Prayer

Dear Lord,

Today I thought of the words of Vincent van Gogh: "It is true there is an ebb and flow, but the sea remains the sea." You are the sea. Although I experience many ups and downs in my emotions and often feel great shifts and changes in my inner life, you remain the same. Your sameness is not the sameness of a rock, but the sameness of a faithful lover. Out of your love I came to life, by your love I am sustained, and to your love I am always called back. There are days of sadness and days of joy; there are feelings of guilt and feelings of gratitude; there are moments of failure and moments of success; but all of them are embraced by your unwavering love. . . . O Lord, sea of love and goodness, let me not fear too much the storms and winds of my daily life, and let me know there is ebb and flow but the sea remains the sea.

Amen.

A Cry for Mercy

SEPTEMBER

Your Inner Community

Those you have deeply loved become part of you. The longer you live, there will always be more people to be loved by you and to become part of your inner community. The wider your inner community becomes, the more easily you will recognize your own brothers and sisters in the strangers around you. . . . The wider the community of your heart, the wider the community around you.

The Inner Voice of Love

Making Room to Welcome Friends

f it is true that solitude diverts us from our fear and anger and makes us empty for a relationship with God, then it is also true that our emptiness provides a very large and sacred space where we can welcome all the people of the world. There is a powerful connection between our emptiness and our ability to welcome. When we give up what sets us apart from others—not just property but also opinions, prejudices, judgments, and mental preoccupations—then we have room within to welcome friends as well as enemies.

Clowning in Rome

God Is Mercy

The older we become, the more we realize how limited we are in our ability to love, how impure our hearts are, and how complex our motivations are. And there is a real temptation to want to look inside of ourselves and clean it all out, and become people with a pure heart, unstained intentions, and unconditional love. Such an attempt is doomed to failure and leads us to ever greater despair. The more we look into ourselves and try to figure ourselves out, the more we become entangled in our own imperfections. Indeed, we cannot save ourselves. Only Jesus can save us. That is why it is so important to remove your inner eye away from the complexities of your own broken heart toward the pure but broken heart of Jesus. Looking at him and his immense mercy will give you the ability to accept your own imperfections and to really let yourself be cared for by the mercy and love of Jesus.

I remember how Thomas Merton once wrote: "God is mercy in mercy in mercy." This means that the more we come to know ourselves, the more we come to know God's mercy, which is beyond the mercy we know. Letting go of the desire to be perfect lovers, and allowing God to love our people through us, that is the great spiritual call that is given to you and to me. There in the pure heart of God, embraced by his unconditional love, you will find the true joy and peace your heart is longing for.

Love, Henri

Praying for God's Mercy

There is probably no prayer in the history of Christianity that has been prayed so frequently and intimately as the prayer "Lord, have mercy." . . . This cry for mercy is possible only when we are willing to confess that somehow, somewhere, we ourselves have something to do with our losses. Crying for mercy is a recognition that blaming God, the world, or others for our losses does not do full justice to the truth of who we are. At the moment we are willing to take responsibility, even for the pain we didn't cause directly, blaming is converted into an acknowledgment of our own role in human brokenness.

The prayer for God's mercy comes from a heart that knows that this human brokenness is not a fatal condition of which we have become the sad victims, but the bitter fruit of the human choice to say no to love.

With Burning Hearts

Let Him Love You

The question of receiving the love of Christ is really very important. I personally feel more and more that sometimes it is harder for us to fully receive love than to give it. I am more and more convinced that we will find the peace and joy of Christ when we let him truly enter into the deepest places of our heart, especially those places where we are afraid, insecure, and self-rejecting.

Love, Henri

Dying Leads to Love

Am I afraid to die? I am every time I let myself be seduced by the noisy voices of my world telling me that my "little life" is all I have and advising me to cling to it with all my might. But when I let these voices move to the background of my life and listen to that small soft voice calling me the Beloved, I know that there is nothing to fear and that dying is the greatest act of love, the act that leads me into the eternal embrace of my God whose love is everlasting.

Life of the Beloved

The Illusion of Immortality

Much violence in our society is based on the illusion of immortality, which is the illusion that life is a property to be defended and not a gift to be shared. When the elderly no longer can bring us in contact with our own aging, we quickly start playing dangerous power games to uphold the illusion of being ageless and immortal. Then, not only will the wisdom of the elderly remain hidden from us, but the elderly themselves will lose their own deepest understanding of life. For who can remain a teacher when there are no students willing to learn?

Aging

Choosing How to Live Death

You and I have to trust that our short little lives can bear fruit far beyond the boundaries of our chronologies. But we have to choose this and trust deeply that we have a spirit to send that will bring joy, peace, and life to those who will remember us. Francis of Assisi died in 1226, but he is still very much alive! His death was a true gift, and today, nearly eight centuries later, he continues to fill his brothers and sisters, within and without the Franciscan orders, with great energy and life. He died, but never died. His spirit keeps descending upon us. More than ever I am convinced that death can, indeed, be chosen as our final gift of life.

Life of the Beloved

Every Bit of Life Is Touched by a Bit of Death

Joy and sadness are as close to each other as the splendid colored leaves of a New England fall to the soberness of barren trees. When you touch the hand of a returning friend, you already know that he will have to leave again. When you are moved by the quiet vastness of a sun-colored ocean, you miss the friend who cannot see the same. Joy and sadness are born at the same time, both arising from such deep places in your heart that you can't find words to capture your complex emotions.

But this intimate experience in which every bit of life is touched by a bit of death can point us beyond the limits of our existence. It can do so by making us look forward in expectation to the day when our hearts will be filled with perfect joy, a joy that no one shall take away from us.

Out of Solitude

The Pressure of Competition

O ne of the saddest aspects of the lives of many students is that they always feel pressured. . . . The word *school,* which comes from *schola* (meaning "free time"), reminds us that schools were originally meant to interrupt a busy existence and create some space to contemplate the mysteries of life. Today they have become the arena for a hectic race to accomplish as much as possible, and to acquire in a short period the necessary things to survive the great battle of human life. Books written to be savored slowly are read hastily to fulfill a requirement, paintings made to be seen with a contemplative eye are taken in as part of a necessary art appreciation course, and music composed to be enjoyed at leisure is listened to in order to identify a period or style. Thus, colleges and universities meant to be places for quiet learning have become places of fierce competition, in which the rewards go to those who produce the most and the best.

Lifesigns

Living Beyond the Success-Failure Syndrome

I hope you stay close to Jesus in the midst of everything. Jesus is, as you know, much more than a story. He is a source of life and is truly able to touch you deeply so that you can go beyond the success-failure syndrome. I really believe that it is possible for you to develop a simple life of prayer that can give you that "holy indifference." By that, I mean the place where you feel so truly safe and so well held that the ups and downs of your life aren't able to distress you or excite you. I have personally found much help in spending a little time every day just repeating in my mind a sacred text such as the prayer of St. Francis, "Make me an instrument of your peace. . . ." When I let these words enter deeply into my consciousness, something new in me happens and I am moved beyond the places where exultation or depression dwell.

Love, Henri

Freedom Is the Goal

Though the forces of evil infecting whole nations and peoples are often hidden, complex, and elusive, we are called, as Christians, to unmask and expel them in the Name of the God of Love. . . .

As long as national security is our primary concern and national survival more important than preserving life on this planet, we continue to live in the house of fear. Ultimately, we must choose between security—individual, social, or national—and freedom.

Freedom is the true human goal. Life is only true if it is free. An obsessive concern for security freezes us; it leads us to rigidity, fixation, and eventually death. The more preoccupied we are with security the more visible the force of death becomes, whether in the form of a pistol beside our bed, a rifle in our house, or a Trident submarine in our port. . . .

We must find a way to go beyond our national security obsession and reach out and foster life for all people, whatever their nationality, race, or religion.

Lifesigns

You Are Home

have been meditating on the story of the prodigal son. It is a story about returning. I realize the importance of returning over and over again. My life drifts away from God. I have to return. My heart moves away from my first love. I have to return. My mind wanders to strange images. I have to return. Returning is a lifelong struggle. . . . I am moved by the fact that the father didn't require any higher motivation. His love was so total and unconditional that he simply welcomed his son home.

The Road to Daybreak

The Rhythm of Nature

This morning John Eudes spoke about autumn as a time of plenitude, a time of fulfillment in which the richness of nature becomes abundantly visible, but also a time in which nature points beyond itself by the fragility of its passing beauty. . . . When I walked out I was overwhelmed by the beauty of the landscape unfolding itself before my eyes. Looking out over the Genesee valley, I was dazzled by the bright colors of the trees. The yellow of the hickory trees, the different shades of red from the maples and oaks, the green of the willows—together they formed a fantastic spectacle. The sky was full of mysterious cloud formations, and just as I walked down to the guesthouse, the sun's rays burst through the clouds and covered the land with their light, making the cornfields look like a golden tapestry.

The beauty of the fall is unbelievable in this part of the country. I can only say with the psalmist: "The hills are girded with joy, they shout for joy, yes, they sing" (see Psalms 65:12–13).

Two weeks from now the colorful leaves will have whirled to the ground and the trees will be bare, announcing the coming of winter and snow. It will only be a few months before all the hills will be white and the green of the winter wheat covered with a thick blanket of frozen snow. But then we can remember the rich powers hidden underneath that will show themselves again to those who have the patience to wait.

The Genesee Diary

Preparing for Death

S ome people say they are afraid of death. Others say they are not. But most people are quite afraid of dying. The slow deterioration of mind and body, the pains of a growing cancer, the ravaging effects of AIDS, becoming a burden for your friends, losing control of your movements, being talked about or spoken to with half-truths, forgetting recent events and the names of visitors—all of that and much more is what we really fear. It's not surprising that we sometimes say: "I hope it doesn't last long. I hope I will die through a sudden heart attack and not after a long, painful illness."

But, whatever we think or hope, the way we will die is unpredictable and our worries about it quite fruitless. Still we need to be prepared. Preparing ourselves for our deaths is the most important task of life, at least when we believe that death is not the total dissolution of our identity but the way to its fullest revelation. Death, as Jesus speaks about it, is that moment in which total defeat and total victory are one. The cross on which Jesus died is the sign of this oneness of defeat and victory. Jesus speaks about his death as being "lifted up."

Here and Now

Befriending Death

Our first task is to befriend death. I like that expression "to befriend." I first heard it used by Jungian analyst James Hillman when he attended a seminar I taught on Christian Spirituality at Yale Divinity School. He emphasized the importance of "befriending": befriending your dreams, befriending your shadow, befriending your unconscious. He made it convincingly clear that in order to become full human beings, we have to claim the totality of our experience; we come to maturity by integrating not only the light but also the dark side of our story into our selfhood. That made a lot of sense to me, since I am quite familiar with my own inclination, and that of others, to avoid, deny, or suppress the painful side of life, a tendency that always leads to physical, mental, or spiritual disaster. . . .

I have a deep sense, hard to articulate, that if we could really befriend death we would be free people. So many of our doubts and hesitations, ambivalences and insecurities are bound up with our deep-seated fear of death that our lives would be significantly different if we could relate to death as a familiar guest instead of as a threatening stranger.

A Letter of Consolation

Facing Our Mortality

To befriend death, we must claim that we are children of God, sisters and brothers of all people, and parents of generations yet to come. In so doing, we liberate our death from its absurdity and make it the gateway to a new life.

In our society, in which childhood is something to grow away from, in which wars and ethnic conflicts constantly mock brotherhood and sisterhood among people, and in which the greatest emphasis is on succeeding in the few years we have, it hardly seems possible that death could be a gateway to anything.

Still, Jesus has opened this way for us. When we choose his way to live and die, we can face our death with the mocking question of the apostle Paul: "Death, where is your victory? Death, where is your sting?" (1 Corinthians 15:55). This is a choice, but a hard choice. The powers of darkness that surround us are strong and easily tempt us to let our fear of death rule our thoughts, words, and actions.

But can we choose to befriend our death as Jesus did? We *can* choose to live as God's beloved children in solidarity with all people, trusting in our ultimate fruitfulness. And in so doing, we can also become people who care for others. As men and women who have faced our mortality, we can help our brothers and sisters to dispel the darkness of death and guide them toward the light of God's grace.

Our Greatest Gift

Suddenly a Wall Becomes a Gate

Death is part of a much greater and much deeper event, the fullness of which we cannot comprehend, but of which we know that it is a life-bringing event. . . . What seemed to be the end proved to be the beginning; what seemed to be a cause for fear proved to be a cause for courage; what seemed to be defeat proved to be victory; and what seemed to be the basis for despair proved to be the basis for hope. Suddenly a wall becomes a gate, and although we are not able to say with much clarity or precision what lies beyond the gate, the tone of all that we do and say on our way to the gate changes drastically.

A Letter of Consolation

A New Vision of Maturity

I find myself with the same old struggles every time I am in a new and unfamiliar milieu. In particular, the experience of isolation keeps returning, not in a lessening but in an increasing degree. Becoming older makes the experience of isolation much more familiar—maybe simply because of sheer repetition—but not less painful.

So maybe the question is not how to cope better, but how slowly to allow my unchanging character to become a way of humility and surrender to God. As I recognize my fears of being left alone and my desire for a sense of belonging, I may gradually give up my attempts to fill my loneliness and be ready to recognize with my heart that God is Emmanuel, "God-with-us," and that I belong to him before anything or anyone else.

And so a new vision of maturity may emerge; not a vision in which I am more and more able to deal with my own pains, but one in which I am more willing to let my Lord deal with them. After all, maturation in a spiritual sense is a growing willingness to stretch out my arms, to have a belt put round me, and to be led where I would rather not go (John 21:18).

Gracias!

The Most Important Choice

f I die with much anger and bitterness, I will leave my family and friends behind in confusion, guilt, shame, or weakness. When I felt my death approaching,* I suddenly realized how much I could influence the hearts of those whom I would leave behind. If I could truly say that I was grateful for what I had lived, eager to forgive and be forgiven, full of hope that those who loved me would continue their lives of joy and peace, and confident that Jesus who calls me would guide all who somehow belonged to my life—if I could do that—I would, in the hour of my death, reveal more true spiritual freedom than I had been able to reveal during all the years of my life. I realize on a very deep level that dying is the most important act of living. It involves a choice to bind others with guilt or to set them free with gratitude.

Beyond the Mirror

---

* Henri Nouwen was in a life-threatening accident in 1989.

Memories of Paradise

know that the fact that I am always searching for God, always struggling to discover the fullness of Love, always yearning for the complete truth, tells me that I have already been given a taste of God, of Love, and of Truth. I can only look for something that I have, to some degree, already found. How can I search for beauty and truth unless that beauty and truth are already known to me in the depth of my heart? It seems that all of us human beings have deep inner memories of the paradise that we have lost. Maybe the word *innocence* is better than the word *paradise.* We were innocent before we started feeling guilty; we were in the light before we entered into the darkness; we were at home before we started to search for a home. Deep in the recesses of our minds and hearts there lies hidden the treasure we seek. We know its preciousness, and we know that it holds the gift we most desire: a life stronger than death.

Life of the Beloved

Presence and Absence

O ne of the mysteries of life is that memory can often bring
us closer to each other than can physical presence. Physical presence not only invites but also blocks communication. In
our pre-resurrection state our bodies hide as much as they reveal. Indeed, many of our disappointments and frustrations in
life are related to the fact that seeing and touching each other
does not always create the closeness we seek. The more experience in living we have, the more we sense that closeness grows
in the continuous interplay between presence and absence.

The Living Reminder

24

We Are Free to Choose

s aging a way to the darkness or a way to the light? It is not given to anyone to make a final judgment, since the answer can only be brought forth from the center of our being. No one can decide for anyone else how his or her aging shall or should be. It belongs to the greatness of men and women that the meaning of their existence escapes the power of calculations and predictions. Ultimately, it can only be discovered and affirmed in the freedom of the heart. There we are able to decide between segregation and unity, between desolation and hope, between loss of self and a new, re-creating vision. Everyone will age and die, but this knowledge has no inherent direction. It can be destructive as well as creative, oppressive as well as liberating.

Aging

Our Weakness Blesses Others

Our weakness and old age call people to surround us and support us. By not resisting weakness and by gratefully receiving another's care we call forth community and provide our caregivers an opportunity to give their own gifts of compassion, care, love, and service. As we are given into their hands, others are blessed and enriched by caring for us. Our weakness bears fruit in their lives.

And dying is our ultimate vulnerability. Instead of looking at the weakness of old age as simply the experience of loss after loss, we can choose it as a passage to emptiness where our hearts have room to be filled with the Spirit of Love overflowing. It is ultimate weakness, but is also potentially the greatest moment of our fruitfulness.

Finding My Way Home

Real Human Grief

Real human grief means allowing the illusion of immortality to die in us. When those whom we love with an "endless love" die, something also has to die within us. If we do not allow this to happen, we will lose touch with reality, our lives will become increasingly artificial, and we will lose our human capacity for compassion.

The Road to Daybreak

A Joyful Vision of Life and Death

Our life is a short opportunity to say yes to God's love. Our death is a full coming home to that love. Do we desire to come home? It seems that most of our efforts are aimed at delaying this homecoming as long as possible.

Writing to the Christians at Philippi, the apostle Paul shows a radically different attitude. He says: "I want to be gone and be with Christ, and this is by far the stronger desire—and yet for your sake to stay alive in this body is a more urgent need." Paul's deepest desire is to be completely united with God through Christ and that desire makes him look at death as a "positive gain." His other desire, however, is to stay alive in the body and fulfill his mission. That will offer him an opportunity for fruitful work.

We are challenged once again to look at our lives from above. When, indeed, Jesus came to offer us full communion with God, by making us partakers of his death and resurrection, what else can we desire but to leave our mortal bodies and so reach the final goal of our existence? The only reason for staying in this valley of tears can be to continue the mission of Jesus who has sent us into the world as his Father sent him into the world. Looking from above, life is a short, often painful mission, full of occasions to do fruitful work for God's kingdom, and death is the open door that leads into the hall of celebration where the king himself will serve us.

It all seems such an upside-down way of being! But it's the way of Jesus and the way for us to follow. There is nothing morbid about it. To the contrary, it's a joyful vision of life and death.

Here and Now

A Death for Others

The great mystery is that all people who have lived with and in the Spirit of God participate through their deaths in the sending of the Spirit. God's love continues to be sent to us, and Jesus' death continues to bear fruit through all whose death is like his death, a death for others.

In this way, dying becomes a way to an everlasting fruitfulness. We touch here the most hope-giving aspect of our death. Our death may be the end of our success, our productivity, our fame, or our importance among people, but it is not the end of our fruitfulness. The opposite is true: the fruitfulness of our lives shows itself in its fullness only after we have died. We ourselves seldom see or experience our fruitfulness. Often we remain too preoccupied with our accomplishments and have no eye for the fruitfulness of what we live. But the beauty of life is that it bears fruit long after life itself has come to an end. Jesus says: "In all truth I tell you, unless a wheat grain falls into the earth and dies, it remains only a single grain; but if it dies, it yields a rich harvest" (John 12:24).

This is the mystery of Jesus' death and of the deaths of all who lived in his Spirit. Their lives yield fruit far beyond the limits of their short and often very localized existence.

Our Greatest Gift

The In-Dwelling of God
Here and Now

Eternal life. Where is it? When is it? For a long time I have thought about eternal life as a life after all my birthdays have run out. For most of my years I have spoken about the eternal life as the "afterlife," as "life after death." But the older I become, the less interest my "afterlife" holds for me. Worrying not only about tomorrow, next year, and the next decade, but even about the next life, seems a false preoccupation. Wondering how things will be for me after I die seems, for the most part, a distraction. When my clear goal is the eternal life, that life must be reachable right now, where I am, because eternal life is life in and with God, and God is where I am here and now.

The great mystery of the spiritual life—the life in God—is that we don't have to wait for it as something that will happen later. Jesus says: "Dwell in me as I dwell in you." It is this divine in-dwelling that is eternal life. It is the active presence of God at the center of my living—the movement of God's Spirit within us—that gives us the eternal life.

Here and Now

A Prayer

O Lord,

Life passes by swiftly. Events that a few years ago kept me totally preoccupied have now become vague memories; conflicts that a few months ago seemed so crucial in my life now seem futile and hardly worth the energy; inner turmoil that robbed me of my sleep only a few weeks ago has now become a strange emotion of the past; books that filled me with amazement a few days ago now do not seem as important; thoughts that kept my mind captive only a few hours ago have now lost their power and have been replaced by others. . . . Why am I continuously trapped in this sense of urgency and emergency? Why do I not see that you are eternal, that your kingdom lasts forever, and that for you a thousand years are like one day? O Lord, let me enter into your presence and there taste the eternal, timeless, everlasting love with which you invite me to let go of my time-bound anxieties, fears, preoccupations, and worries. . . . Lord, teach me your ways and give me the courage to follow them.

Amen.

A Cry for Mercy

OCTOBER

The Freedom of the Children of God

We are fearful people. We are afraid of conflict, war, an uncertain future, illness, and, most of all, death. This fear takes away our freedom and gives our society the power to manipulate us with threats and promises. When we can reach beyond our fears to the One who loves us with a love that was there before we were born and will be there after we die, then oppression, persecution, and even death will be unable to take our freedom. Once we have come to the deep inner knowledge—a knowledge more of the heart than of the mind—that we are born out of love and will die into love, that every part of our being is deeply rooted in love, and that this love is our true Father and Mother, then all forms of evil, illness, and death lose their final power over us and become painful but hopeful reminders of our true divine childhood. The apostle Paul expressed this experience of the complete freedom of the children of God when he wrote, "I am certain of this: neither death nor life, nor angels, nor principalities, nothing already in existence and nothing still to come, nor any power, nor the heights nor the depths, nor any created thing whatever, will be able to come between us and the love of God, known to us in Christ Jesus" (Romans 8:38–39).

Our Greatest Gift

Live Confidently

While Jesus predicts that people will die of fear "as they await what menaces the world" (Luke 21:26), he says to his followers: "Stay awake, praying at all times for the strength to survive all that is going to happen, and to stand with confidence before the Son of Man" (Luke 21:36). After I gazed for a long time at [Andrei] Rublev's Trinity [icon] these words spoke to me with new power, "Praying at all times" has come to mean "dwelling in the house of God all the days of our lives." "Surviving all that is going to happen" now tells me that I no longer need to be victim of the fear, hatred, and violence that rule the world. "Standing with confidence before the Son of Man" no longer just refers to the end of time, but opens for me the possibility of living confidently, that is, with trust (the literal meaning of *con-fide*) in the midst of hostility and violence.

Behold the Beauty of the Lord

Accept Your Identity as a Child of God

Your true identity is as a child of God. This is the identity you have to accept. Once you have claimed it and settled in it, you can live in a world that gives you much joy as well as pain. You can receive the praise as well as the blame that comes to you as an opportunity for strengthening your basic identity, because the identity that makes you free is anchored beyond all human praise and blame. You belong to God, and it is as a child of God that you are sent into the world.

The Inner Voice of Love

God's First Love

Knowing God's heart means consistently, radically, and very concretely to announce and reveal that God is love and only love, and that every time fear, isolation, or despair begin to invade the human soul this is not something that comes from God. This sounds very simple and maybe even trite, but very few people know that they are loved without any conditions or limits.

This unconditional and unlimited love is what the evangelist John calls God's first love. "Let us love," he says, "because God loved us first" (1 John 4:19). The love that often leaves us doubtful, frustrated, angry, and resentful is the second love, that is to say, the affirmation, affection, sympathy, encouragement, and support we receive from our parents, teachers, spouses, and friends. We all know how limited, broken, and very fragile that love is. Behind the many expressions of this second love there is always the chance of rejection, withdrawal, punishment, blackmail, violence, and even hatred. . . .

The radical good news is that the second love is only a broken reflection of the first love and that the first love is offered to us by a God in whom there are no shadows. Jesus' heart is the incarnation of the shadow-free first love of God.

In the Name of Jesus

6
—

The Joy of Belonging

We have heard the story of the encounter between Jesus and Mary of Magdala, two people who love each other. Jesus says, "Mary." She recognizes him and says, " 'Rabboni,' " which means Master" (John 20:16). This simple and deeply moving story brings me in touch with my fear as well as my desire to be known. . . . Often I am tempted to think that I am loved only as I remain partially unknown. I fear that the love I receive is conditional and then say to myself, "If they really knew me, they would not love me." But when Jesus calls Mary by name he speaks to her entire being. She realizes that the One who knows her most deeply is not moving away from her, but is coming to her offering her his unconditional love. . . . Mary feels at once fully known and fully loved. The division between what she feels safe to show and what she does not dare to reveal no longer exists. She is fully seen and she knows that the eyes that see her are the eyes of forgiveness, mercy, love, and unconditional acceptance. . . . What a joy to be fully known and fully loved at the same time! It is the joy of belonging through Jesus to God and being fully safe and fully free.

The Road to Daybreak

Power Through Powerlessness

The movement from power through strength to power through powerlessness is our call. As fearful, anxious, insecure, and wounded people we are tempted constantly to grab a little bit of power that the world around us offers, left and right, here and there, now and then. These bits of power make us little puppets jerked up and down on strings until we are dead. But insofar as we dare to be baptized in powerlessness, always moving toward the poor who do not have such power, we are plunged right into the heart of God's endless mercy. We are free to reenter our world with the same divine power with which Jesus came, and we are able to walk in the valley of darkness and tears, unceasingly in communion with God, with our heads erect, confidently standing under the cross of our life.

It is this power that engenders leaders for our communities, women and men who dare to take risks and take new initiatives. It is this power that enables us to be not only gentle as doves, but also as clever as serpents in our dealings with governments and church agencies. It is this power that enables us to talk straight and without hesitation about sharing money with those who have financial resources, to call men and women to radical service, to challenge people to make long-term commitments in the world of human services, and to keep announcing the good news everywhere at all times. It is this divine power that makes us saints—fearless—who can make all things new.

Finding My Way Home

8

Divine Forgiveness

I have often said, "I forgive you," but even as I said these words
my heart remained angry or resentful. I still wanted to hear
the story that I was right after all; I still wanted to hear apologies and excuses; I still wanted the satisfaction of receiving some
praise in return—if only the praise for being so forgiving!

But God's forgiveness is unconditional; it comes from a heart
that does not demand anything of itself, a heart that is completely empty of self-seeking. It is this divine forgiveness that I
have to practice in my daily life. It calls me to keep stepping over
all my arguments that say forgiveness is unwise, unhealthy, and
impractical. It challenges me to step over all my needs for gratitude and compliments. Finally, it demands of me that I step over
that wounded part of my heart that feels hurt and wronged and
that wants to stay in control and put a few conditions between
me and the one whom I am asked to forgive. . . . Only when
I remember that I am the Beloved Child can I welcome those
who want to return with the same compassion as that with
which the Father welcomes me.

The Return of the Prodigal Son

Live Your Wounds

You have been wounded in many ways. The more you open yourself to being healed, the more you will discover how deep your wounds are. . . . The great challenge is living your wounds through instead of thinking them through. It is better to cry than to worry, better to feel your wounds deeply than to understand them, better to let them enter into your silence than to talk about them. The choice you face constantly is whether you are taking your hurts to your head or to your heart. In your head you can analyze them, find their causes and consequences, and coin words to speak and write about them. But no final healing is likely to come from that source. You need to let your wounds go down to your heart. Then you can live through them and discover that they will not destroy you. Your heart is greater than your wounds.

The Inner Voice of Love

Befriend Your Pain

I want to say to you that most of our brokenness cannot be simply taken away. It's there. And the deepest pain that you and I suffer is often the pain that stays with us all our lives. It cannot be simply solved, fixed, done away with. . . . What are we then told to do with that pain, with that brokenness, that anguish, that agony that continually rises up in our heart? We are called to embrace it, to befriend it. To not just push it away . . . to walk right over it, to ignore it. No, to embrace it, to befriend it, and say that is my pain and I claim my pain as the way God is willing to show me his love.

"Life of the Spirit"

Detach from the Past

I am increasingly convinced that it is possible to live the wounds of the past not as gaping abysses that cannot be fulfilled and, therefore, keep threatening us as gateways to new life. The "gateless gate" of Zen and the "healing wounds of Christ" both encourage us to detach ourselves from the past and trust in the glory to which we are called.

Sabbatical Journey

Deciding to Be Grateful

Gratitude is the most fruitful way of deepening your consciousness that you are not an "accident," but a divine choice. It is important to realize how often we have had chances to be grateful and have not used them. When someone is kind to us, when an event turns out well, when a problem is solved, a relationship restored, a wound healed, there are very concrete reasons to offer thanks: be it with words, with flowers, with a letter, a card, a phone call, or just a gesture of affection. . . . Every time we decide to be grateful it will be easier to see new things to be grateful for. Gratitude begets gratitude, just as love begets love.

Life of the Beloved

The Grateful Life

How can we live a truly grateful life? When we look back at all that has happened to us, we easily divide our lives into good things to be grateful for and bad things to forget. But with a past thus divided, we cannot move freely into the future. With many things to forget we can only limp toward the future.

True spiritual gratitude embraces all of our past, the good as well as the bad events, the joyful as well as the sorrowful moments. From the place where we stand, everything that took place brought us to this place, and we want to remember all of it as part of God's guidance. That does not mean that all that happened in the past was good, but it does mean that even the bad didn't happen outside the loving presence of God. . . . Once all of our past is remembered in gratitude, we are free to be sent into the world to proclaim good news to others.

Here and Now

The Great Event of Salvation

To live a life in the memory of Jesus Christ means first of all that that memory is a healing memory. How does the memory of Jesus Christ heal? The memory of Jesus Christ heals because it lifts up our small life and brings it in connection with a much larger event. As Christians, we are participating in a memory that goes far, far back to that great moment when God himself entered into history and shared the human condition. When our little history can be connected with the great history of salvation a tremendous change starts taking place because our little pains and our little joys are no longer just little pains and little joys but they point beyond themselves . . . to a great event of salvation of which we have become a part. . . . Our lives can be healed by the memory of the incarnation and the story of salvation.

The Christ-Memory in Our Lives

Choosing a Life of Contrition

Celebrating the Eucharist requires that we stand in this world accepting our co-responsibility for the evil that surrounds and pervades us. As long as we remain stuck in our complaints about the terrible times in which we live and the terrible situations we have to bear and the terrible fate we have to suffer, we can never come to contrition. And contrition can grow only out of a contrite heart. When our losses are pure fate, our gains are pure luck! Fate does not lead to contrition, nor luck to gratitude.

Indeed, the conflicts in our personal lives as well as the conflicts on regional, national, or world scales are our conflicts, and only by claiming responsibility for them can we move beyond them—choosing a life of forgiveness, peace, and love.

With Burning Hearts

Suffering

The poor we see every day, the stories about deportation, torture, and murder we hear every day, and the undernourished children we touch every day, reveal to us the suffering Christ has hidden within us. When we allow this image of the suffering Christ within us to grow to its full maturity, then ministry to the poor and oppressed becomes a real possibility; because then we can indeed hear, see, and touch him within us as well as among us. . . . Once we have seen the suffering Christ within us, we will see him wherever we see people in pain. Once we have seen the suffering Christ among us, we will recognize him in our innermost self. Thus we come to experience that the first commandment, to love God with all your heart, with all your soul, and with all your mind, resembles indeed the second: "You must love your neighbor as yourself" (Matthew 22:39–40).

Gracias!

To Care

To care one must offer one's own vulnerable self to others as a source of healing. To care for the aging, therefore, means first of all to enter into close contact with your own aging self, to sense your own time, and to experience the movements of your own life cycle. From this aging self, healing can come forth and others can be invited to cast off the paralyzing fear for their future. As long as we think that caring means only being nice and friendly to old people, paying them a visit, bringing them a flower, or offering them a ride, we are apt to forget how much more important it is for us to be willing and able to be present to those we care for. And how can we be fully present to the elderly when we are hiding from our own aging? How can we listen to their pains when their stories open wounds in us that we are trying to cover up? How can we offer companionship when we want to keep our own aging self out of the room, and how can we gently touch the vulnerable spots in old people's lives when we have armored our own vulnerable self with fear and blindness? Only when we enter into solidarity with the aging and speak out of common experience, can we help others to discover the freedom of old age.

Aging

Real Care

The great secret of the spiritual life, the life of the Beloved Sons and Daughters of God, is that everything we live, be it gladness or sadness, joy or pain, health or illness, can all be part of the journey toward the full realization of our humanity. It is not hard to say to one another: "All that is good and beautiful leads us to the glory of the children of God." But it is very hard to say: "But didn't you know that we all have to suffer and thus enter into our glory?" Nonetheless, real care means the willingness to help each other in making our brokenness into a gateway to joy.

Life of the Beloved

Life Is Precious

The beauty and preciousness of life is intimately linked with its fragility and mortality. We can experience that every day—when we take a flower in our hands, when we see a butterfly dance in the air, when we caress a little baby. Fragility and giftedness are both there, and our joy is connected with both.

With Burning Hearts

Passionately in Love with God

All the great saints in history about whom I have read have been people who were so passionately in love with God that they were completely free to love other people in a deep, affective way, without any strings attached. True charity is gratuitous love, a love that gives gratuitously and receives gratuitously. It is following the first commandment that asks us to give everything we have to God and that makes the second commandment truly possible. . . .

We are touching here on the source of much of the suffering in our contemporary society. We have such a need for love that we often expect from our fellow human beings something that only God can give, and then we quickly end up being angry, resentful, lustful, and sometimes even violent. As soon as the first commandment is no longer truly the first, our society moves to the edge of self-destruction.

Love, Henri

Receive Jesus' Love

Jesus wants us to receive the love he offers. He wants nothing more than that we allow him to love us and enjoy that love. This is so hard since we always feel that we have to deserve the love offered to us. But Jesus wants to offer that love to us not because we have earned it, but because he has decided to love us independently of any effort on our side. Our own love for each other should flow from that "first love" that is given to us undeserved.

The Road to Daybreak

Be a Real Friend

True friendships are lasting because true love is eternal. A friendship in which heart speaks to heart is a gift from God, and no gift that comes from God is temporary or occasional. All that comes from God participates in God's eternal life. Love between people, when given by God, is stronger than death. In this sense, true friendships continue beyond the boundary of death. When you have loved deeply that love can grow even stronger after the death of the person you love. This is the core message of Jesus.

When Jesus died, the disciples' friendship with him did not diminish. On the contrary, it grew. This is what the sending of the Spirit was all about. The Spirit of Jesus made Jesus' friendship with his disciples everlasting, stronger, and more intimate than before his death. That is what Paul experienced when he said, "It is no longer I, but Christ living in me" (Galatians 2:20).

You have to trust that every true friendship has no end, that a communion of saints exists among all those, living and dead, who have truly loved God and one another. You know from experience how real this is. Those you have loved deeply and who have died live on in you, not just as memories but as real presences.

Dare to love and be a real friend. The love you give and receive is a reality that will lead you closer and closer to God as well as to those whom God has given you to love.

The Inner Voice of Love

Nurturing Friendship

Friendship requires a constant willingness to forgive each other for not being Christ and a willingness to ask Christ himself to be the true center. When Christ does not mediate a relationship, that relationship easily becomes demanding, manipulating, oppressive, an arena for many forms of rejection. An unmediated friendship cannot last long; you simply expect too much of the other and cannot offer the other the space he or she needs to grow. Friendship requires closeness, affection, support, and mutual encouragement, but also distance, space to grow, freedom to be different, and solitude. To nurture both aspects of a relationship, we must experience a deeper and more lasting affirmation than any human relationship can offer.

The Road to Daybreak

Giving in Friendship

When we truly love God and share in his glory, our relationships lose their compulsive character. We reach out to people not just to receive their affirmations but also to allow them to participate in the love we have come to know through Jesus. Thus true friendship becomes an expression of a greater love.

It is hard work to remind each other constantly of the truth, but it is worth the effort. Constant mutual forgiveness and a continual openness to the love of God are the disciplines that allow us to grow together in friendship.

The Road to Daybreak

A Forgiven Person Forgives

M aybe the reason it seems hard for me to forgive others is that I do not fully believe that I am a forgiven person. If I could fully accept the truth that I am forgiven and do not have to live in guilt or shame, I would really be free. My freedom would allow me to forgive others seventy times seven times. By not forgiving, I chain myself to a desire to get even, thereby losing my freedom. A forgiven person forgives. This is what we proclaim when we pray "and forgive us our trespasses as we forgive those who have trespassed against us."

This lifelong struggle lies at the heart of the Christian life.

The Road to Daybreak

The Burden of Judgment

magine having no need at all to judge anybody. Imagine having no desire to decide whether someone is a good or bad person. Imagine being completely free from the feeling that you have to make up your mind about the morality of someone's behavior. Imagine that you could say: "I am judging no one!"

Imagine—Wouldn't that be true inner freedom? . . . But we can only let go of the heavy burden of judging others when we don't mind carrying the light burden of being judged!

Can we free ourselves from the need to judge others? Yes, by claiming for ourselves the truth that we are the Beloved Daughters and Sons of God. As long as we continue to live as if we are what we do, what we have, and what other people think about us, we will remain filled with judgments, opinions, evaluations, and condemnations. We will remain addicted to the need to put people and things in their "right" place. To the degree that we embrace the truth that our identity is not rooted in our success, power, or popularity, we can let go of our need to judge. "Do not judge and you will not be judged; because the judgments you give are the judgments you will get" (Matthew 7:1).

Here and Now

Eyes of Compassion

My recent illness has really convinced me of the importance of not judging or condemning, not even our own past, and of looking at people with immense compassion and love in the way Jesus looked at the adulterous woman and made her discover her own goodness through the eyes of Jesus and thus find the strength to "sin no more."

Love, Henri

A Hidden Hope

The world lies in the power of the evil one. The world does not recognize the light that shines in the darkness. It never did; it never will. But there are people who, in the midst of the world, live with the knowledge that he is alive and dwells within us, that he has overcome the power of death and opens the way to glory. Are there people who come together, who come around the table and do what he did, in memory of him? Are there people who keep telling each other the stories of hope and, together, go out to care for their fellow human beings, not pretending to solve all problems, but to bring a smile to a dying man and a little hope to a lonely child?

It is so little, so unspectacular, yes, so hidden, this Eucharistic life, but it is like yeast, like a mustard seed, like a smile on a baby's face. It is what keeps faith, hope, and love alive in a world that is constantly on the brink of self-destruction.

With Burning Hearts

Hope at All Times

t is central in the biblical tradition that God's love for his people should not be forgotten. It should remain with us in the present. When everything is dark, when we are surrounded by despairing voices, when we do not see any exits, then we can find salvation in a remembered love, a love that is not simply a wistful recollection of a bygone past but a living force that sustains us in the present. Through memory, love transcends the limits of time and offers hope at any moment of our lives.

The Living Reminder

Turn Your Mourning into Dancing

I realize how deeply the death of a parent touches us. We suddenly realize that some of the most intimate ties are broken and that we are called to let our parents move away from us and their place in history.

And still I also believe that absence might lead to the awareness of a new presence. Lately, I have found much comfort in the words of Jesus: "It is for your good that I leave, because unless I leave my Spirit cannot come." Jesus' leaving meant that he would become more intimately present to us, that he would unite himself in a new way with us. Because of his death we can say: "Not I live but Christ lives in me." I have a feeling that this is not just true of Jesus, but in and through Jesus of all people who leave us. In their absence we can develop a new intimacy with them and grow. We even can become more like them and fulfill their mission in life until the day comes that we too have to leave so that our spirit can stay with those we love. In this way mourning can slowly turn into joy, and grief into rebirth.

Love, Henri

A Prayer

Dear God,

I am full of wishes,
full of desires,
full of expectations.
Some of them may be realized, many may not,
but in the midst of all my satisfactions
and disappointments,
I hope in you.
I know that you will never leave me alone
and will fulfill your divine promises.
Even when it seems that things are not going my way,
I know that they are going your way
and that in the end your way is the
best way for me.
O Lord, strengthen my hope,
especially when my many wishes are not fulfilled.
Let me never forget that your name is Love.

Amen.

With Open Hands

NOVEMBER

Saintly Counselors

In the past, the saints had very much moved to the background of my consciousness. During the last few months, they re-entered my awareness as powerful guides on the way to God. I read the lives of many saints and great spiritual men and women, and it seems that they have become real members of my spiritual family, always present to offer suggestions, ideas, advice, consolation, courage, and strength. It is very hard to keep your heart and mind directed toward God when there are no examples to help you in your struggle. Without saints you easily settle for less-inspiring people and quickly follow the ways of others who for a while seem exciting but who are not able to offer lasting support. I am happy to have been able to restore my relationship with many great saintly men and women in history who, by their lives and works, can be real counselors to me.

The Genesee Diary

Remembering the Dead

To remember my mother does not mean telling her story over and over again to my friends, nor does it mean pictures on the wall or a stone on her grave; it does not even mean constantly thinking about her. No. It means making her a participant in God's ongoing work of redemption by allowing her to dispel in me a little more of my darkness and lead me a little closer to the light. In these weeks of mourning she died in me more and more every day, making it impossible for me to cling to her as my mother. Yet by letting her go I did not lose her. Rather, I found that she is closer to me than ever. In and through the Spirit of Christ, she indeed is becoming a part of my very being.

In Memoriam

Claiming the Light

People who have come to know the joy of God do not deny the darkness, but they choose not to live in it. They claim that the light that shines in the darkness can be trusted more than the darkness itself and that a little bit of light can dispel a lot of darkness. They point each other to flashes of light here and there, and remind each other that they reveal the hidden but real presence of God. They discover that there are people who heal each other's wounds, forgive each other's offenses, share their possessions, foster the spirit of community, celebrate the gifts they have received, and live in constant anticipation of the full manifestation of God's glory.

The Return of the Prodigal Son

4

Love Remembers

I t is possible to have intimate relationships with loved ones who have died. Death sometimes deepens the intimacy. . . . [I believe] that after separation certain people continue to be very significant for us in our hearts and through our memories. Remembering them is much more than just thinking of them, because we are making them part of our members, part of our whole being.

Knowing this experience allows me to live from the deep belief that I have love to offer to people, not only here, but also beyond my short, little life. I am a human being who was loved by God before I was born and whom God will love after I die. This brief lifetime is my opportunity to receive love, deepen love, grow in love, and give love. When I die love continues to be active, and from full communion with God I am present by love to those I leave behind.

Finding My Way Home

Mourning as a Path to Freedom

I am deeply convinced that the death of those whom we love always is a death for us, that is to say, a death that calls us to deepen our own basic commitment and to develop a new freedom to proclaim what we most believe in. Mourning is a process in which you were, so to say, freed from old bonds, but in which new bonds, more spiritual bonds, are being made.

Love, Henri

The Unifying Love of God

When your deepest self is connected with the deepest self of another, that person's absence may be painful, but it will lead you to a profound communion with the person, because loving each other is loving in God. When the place where God dwells in you is intimately connected with the place where God dwells in the other, the absence of the other person is not destructive. On the contrary, it will challenge you to enter more deeply into communion with God, the source of all unity and community among people.

The Inner Voice of Love

The Fellowship of the Weak

F ear, shame, and guilt often make us stay in our isolation and prevent us from realizing that our handicap, whatever it is, can always become the way to an intimate and healing fellowship in which we come to know one another as humans.

After all, everyone shares the handicap of mortality. Our individual, physical, emotional, and spiritual failures are but symptoms of this disease. Only when we use these symptoms of mortality to form a fellowship of the weak can hope emerge. It is in the confession of our brokenness that the real strength of new and everlasting life can be affirmed and made visible.

Gracias!

Willing Love

Love among people is not first of all a feeling or an emotion or a sentiment but a decision of the will to be faithful to each other. . . . There are really no people whom we can love with unlimited feelings of love. We are all imperfect, broken, sinful people, but we are able to love one another because we are able to will to be faithful and constantly forgive each other's unfaithfulness.

Love, Henri

Passages to New Life

One of the most radical demands for you and me is the discovery of our lives as a series of movements or passages. When we are born, we leave our mothers' womb for the larger, brighter world of the family. It changes everything, and there is no going back. When we go to school, we leave our homes and families and move to a larger community of people where our lives are forever larger and more expansive. Later when our children are grown and they ask us for more space and freedom than we can offer, our lives may seem less meaningful. It all keeps changing. When we grow older, we retire or lose our jobs, and everything shifts again. It seems as though we are always passing from one phase to the next, gaining and losing someone, some place, something.

You live all these passages in an environment where you are constantly tempted to be destroyed by resentment, by anger, and by a feeling of being put down. The losses remind you constantly that all isn't perfect and it doesn't always happen for you the way you expected; that perhaps you had hoped events would not have been so painful, but they were; or that you expected something from certain relationships that never materialized. You find yourself disillusioned with the irrevocable personal losses: your health, your lover, your job, your hope, your dream. Your whole life is filled with losses, endless losses. And every time there are losses there are choices to be made. You choose to live your losses as passages to anger, blame, hatred, depression, and resentment, or you choose to let these losses be passages to something new, something wider, and deeper. The question is not how to avoid loss and make it not happen, but how to choose it as a passage, as an exodus to greater life and freedom.

The Blessing Hidden in Grief

What to do with our losses? . . . We must mourn our losses. We cannot talk or act them away, but we can shed tears over them and allow ourselves to grieve deeply. To grieve is to allow our losses to tear apart feelings of security and safety and lead us to the painful truth of our brokenness. Our grief makes us experience the abyss of our own life in which nothing is settled, clear, or obvious, but everything is constantly shifting and changing. . . . But in the midst of all this pain, there is a strange, shocking, yet very surprising voice. It is the voice of the One who says: "Blessed are those who mourn; they shall be comforted." That's the unexpected news: there is a blessing hidden in our grief. Not those who comfort are blessed, but those who mourn! Somehow, in the midst of our tears, a gift is hidden. Somehow, in the midst of our mourning, the first steps of the dance take place. Somehow, the cries that well up from our losses belong to our songs of gratitude.

With Burning Hearts

Choosing Joy

I am convinced we can choose joy. Every moment we decide to respond to an event or a person with joy instead of sadness. When we truly believe that God is life and only life, then nothing need have the power to draw us into the sad realm of death. To choose joy does not mean to choose happy feelings or an artificial atmosphere of hilarity. But it does mean the determination to let whatever takes place bring us one step closer to the God of life.

Maybe this is what is so important about quiet moments of meditation and prayer. They allow me to take a critical look at my moods and to move from victimization to free choice.

The Road to Daybreak

Cup of Sorrow, Cup of Joy

When we are crushed like grapes, we cannot think of the wine we will become. The sorrow overwhelms us, makes us throw ourselves on the ground, facedown, and sweat drops of blood. Then we need to be reminded that our cup of sorrow is also our cup of joy and that one day we will be able to taste the joy as fully as we now taste the sorrow.

Can You Drink the Cup?

Being a Peacemaker

This morning Jonas and I read in the Gospel Jesus' words:
"If you are bringing your gift to the altar, and there you
remember that your brother or sister has something against you,
leave your gift in front of the altar; go at once and make peace
with your brother, and then come back and offer your gift"
(Matthew 5:23–24). . . . As I think about Jesus' words, I know
that I must let go of all divisive emotions and thoughts so that I
can truly experience peace with all of God's people. This means
an unrestrained willingness to forgive and let go of old fears,
bitterness, resentment, anger, and lust, and thus find reconciliation.

In this way I can be a real peacemaker. My inner peace can
be a source of peace for all I meet. I can then offer gifts on the
altar of God as a testimony to this peace with my brothers and
sisters.

The Road to Daybreak

Inner Peace and Social Action

While I was traveling through the United States and lecturing about Central America, I became aware that while I was exhausting myself to prevent war, the chances of war were increasing. This has helped me to realize that sometimes the powers of evil seduce us to work for peace in such a way that we come close to losing our soul. Peace Pilgrim helped me see how important inner peace is.[*] It is that sense of God's presence in our lives that allows us to trust in the power of God's peace even when we do little. Living in L'Arche[†] with the handicapped also opened my eyes to the peace that does not belong to this world but can be found here already.

Be sure to make this inner peace your utmost priority. . . . When we radiate the peace of Christ we are peacemakers, and then our peace action can witness to this inner peace. But without that inner peace our actions easily become instruments of the powers of war and destruction.

Jesus' words "Pray unceasingly for the strength to survive all that is going to happen and to stand with confidence before the Son of Man" (Luke 21:36) are of crucial importance for us in these days. Prayer should be our first concern. Without prayer even our "good busyness" will lead us to our destruction.

Love, Henri

---

[*] Peace Pilgrim (1908–1981), born Mildred Lisette Norman, was an American nondenominational spiritual teacher, mystic, pacifist, and peace activist.

[†] See footnote on June 5.

God Is at Work in the World

We have to learn how to think about the events of the day that take place in our community or in our larger world, and to see them as ways to come to know God in new ways. There is the spiritual life and the political world and the economic world, but somehow we must really believe that God is a God of history who works in the events of the day. . . . It is important that you learn to read the newspaper with a heart that sees God at work among his people and to be aware of the great struggle in which you are involved—struggles with the power of evil and the hidden love of God. God is present, but you have to be in touch with that very reality. . . . You might know about Ireland, and Iran and Iraq, and know about communities in different places that suffer . . . but do not see them as a set of distracting things but see God is at work in this world. The world and the reality of daily events are there to be read with the mind and heart of God.

Prayer itself should gradually become more and more reality-oriented. To pray is not to sit there and fantasize and daydream. To pray is to look at Jesus who is real and to believe more and more. The greatest of all reality is the presence of God in the world. God is the core reality from which all things derive their reality. What is not real does not belong to God.

"Personal Growth"

A Gentle and Humble Heart

God's question is: "Are you reading the signs of your time as signs asking you to repent and be converted?" What really counts is our willingness to let the immense sufferings of our brothers and sisters free us from all arrogance and from all judgments and condemnations and give us a heart as gentle and humble as the heart of Jesus.

Here and Now

Acting in God's Name

The first questions are not "How much do we do?" or "How many people do we help out?" but "Are we interiorly at peace?"... Jesus' actions flowed from his interior communion with God. His presence was healing, and it changed the world. In a sense he didn't do anything! "Everyone who touched him was healed" (Mark 6:56)....

When we love God with all our heart, mind, strength, and soul, we cannot do other than love our neighbor, and our very selves. It is in being fully rooted in the heart of God that we are creatively connected with our neighbor as well as with our deepest self. In the heart of God we can see that the other human beings who live on this earth with us are also God's sons and daughters, and belong to the same family we do. There, too, I can recognize and claim my own belovedness, and celebrate with my neighbors.

Our society thinks economically: "How much love do I give to God, how much to my neighbor, and how much to myself?" But God says, "Give all your love to me, and I will give to you, your neighbor, and yourself."

We are not talking here about moral obligations or ethical imperatives. We are talking about the mystical life. It is the intimate communion with God that reveals to us how to live in the world and act in God's Name.

Sabbatical Journey

Recognizing the Gifts of the Poor

I am deeply convinced that we can only work for the liberation of the people if we love them deeply. And we can only love them deeply when we recognize their gift to us. I am deeply convinced of the importance of social change and of the necessity to work hard to bring about a just and peaceful society. But I also feel that this task can only be done in a spirit of gratitude and joy. That is why I am more and more convinced of the importance to live in the Spirit of the Risen Christ. Christ is the God who entered into solidarity with our struggles and became truly a God-with-us. It was this solidarity that led him to the cross by which he overcame death and evil. Believing in the Risen Lord means believing that in and through Christ the evil one has been overcome and that death no longer is the final word. Working for social change, to me, means to make visible in time and place that which has already been accomplished in principle by God himself. This makes it possible to struggle for a better world not out of frustration, resentment, anger, or self-righteousness, but out of care, love, forgiveness, and gratitude.

Love, Henri

Caring for the Dying

Caring for others is, first of all, helping them to overcome that enormous temptation of self-rejection. Whether we are rich or poor, famous or unknown, fully abled or disabled, we all share the fear of being left alone and abandoned, a fear that remains hidden under the surface of our self-composure. It is rooted much more deeply than in the possibility of not being liked or loved by people. Its deepest root lies in the possibility of not being loved at all, of not belonging to anything that lasts, or being swallowed up by a dark nothingness—yes, of being abandoned by God.

Caring, therefore, is being present to people as they fight this ultimate battle, a battle that becomes evermore real and intense as death approaches. Dying and death always call forth, with renewed power, the fear that we are unloved and will, finally, be reduced to useless ashes. To care is to stand by a dying person and to be a living reminder that the person is indeed the beloved child of God. . . .

We shouldn't try to care by ourselves. Care is not an endurance test. We should, whenever possible, care together with others. It is the community of care that reminds the dying person of his or her belovedness.

Our Greatest Gift

Why Pray?

Why should I spend an hour in prayer when I do nothing during that time but think about people I am angry with, people who are angry with me, books I should read, and books I should write, and thousands of other silly things that happen to grab my mind for a moment?

The answer is: because God is greater than my mind and my heart and what is really happening in the house of prayer is not measurable in terms of human success and failure.

What I must do first of all is to be faithful. If I believe that the first commandment is to love God with my whole heart, mind, and soul, then I should at least be able to spend one hour a day with nobody else but God. The question as to whether it is helpful, useful, practical, or fruitful is completely irrelevant, since the only reason to love is love itself. Everything else is secondary.

The remarkable thing, however, is that sitting in the presence of God for one hour each morning—day after day, week after week, month after month—in total confusion and with myriad distractions radically changes my life. God, who loves me so much that he sent his only son not to condemn me but to save me, does not leave me waiting in the dark too long. I might think that each hour is useless, but after thirty or sixty or ninety such useless hours, I gradually realize that I was not as alone as I thought; a very small, gentle voice has been speaking to me far beyond my noisy place.

So, be confident and trust in the Lord.

The Road to Daybreak

Waste Some Time with God

In our utilitarian culture, where we suffer from a collective compulsion to do something practical, helpful, or useful, and where we feel compelled to make a contribution that can give us a sense of worth, contemplative prayer is a form of radical criticism. It is not useful or practical. It is simply to waste time for and with God. It cuts a hole in our busyness and reminds us and others that it is God and not we who creates and sustains the world.

Clowning in Rome

Fools for Christ

Sometimes we have to dare to be fools for Christ. That means that sometimes we have to be willing to give food to people who don't really need or deserve it. And sometimes we have to be willing to work with some people who might even exploit us. Maybe this is as close as we can come to an experience of self-emptying. It is the experience of being useless in the presence of the Lord.

Understand me well, I am not trying to praise impracticality, nor am I trying to suggest that you should not stop doing the things you are doing when they prove to be counterproductive, but I am saying if you come in touch with the experience of being used or the experience of being useless, you might in fact be close to a true Christian experience, or closer than you sought.

Love, Henri

Reflect the Peace of Christic

M aybe you should make a prayer room in your house . . .
a place where you can go and often return and let God
speak to you. . . .

Never forget the words "In this world you will have troubles
but be brave: I have overcome the world." Every time you spend
silent time in your prayer room you celebrate Christ's victory
over the world (over death, over the evil one) and allow yourself
to taste already now the peace that comes from this victory.

It is so important for the people around you to see that peace
of Christ reflected in your eyes, your hands, and your words.
There is more power in that than in all your teaching and or-
ganizing. That is the truth we need to keep telling each other.

Love, Henri

Holy Silence

At first silence might only frighten us. In silence we start hearing voices of darkness: our jealousy and anger, our resentment and desire for revenge, our lust and greed, and our pain over losses, abuses, and rejections. These voices are often noisy and boisterous. They may even deafen us. Our most spontaneous reaction is to run away from them and return to our entertainment.

But if we have the discipline to stay put and not let these dark voices intimidate us, they will gradually lose their strength and recede into the background, creating space for the softer, gentler voices of the light.

These voices speak of peace, kindness, gentleness, goodness, joy, hope, forgiveness, and most of all, love. They might at first seem small and insignificant, and we may have a hard time trusting them. However, they are very persistent and they will be stronger if we keep listening. They come from a very deep place and from very far. They have been speaking to us since before we were born, and they reveal to us that there is no darkness in the One who sent us into the world, only light. They are part of God's voice calling us from all eternity: "My beloved child, my favorite one, my joy."

Can You Drink the Cup?

Silence and Speaking Belong Together

To know ourselves truly and acknowledge fully our own unique journey, we need to be known and acknowledged by others for who we are. We cannot live a spiritual life in secrecy. We cannot find our way to true freedom in isolation. Silence without speaking is as dangerous as solitude without community. They belong together.

Can You Drink the Cup?

Community Makes God Visible

Nothing is sweet or easy about community. Community is a fellowship of people who do not hide their joys and sorrows but make them visible to each other as a gesture of hope. In community we say: "Life is full of gains and losses, joys and sorrows, ups and downs—but we do not have to live it alone. We want to drink our cup together and thus celebrate the truth that the wounds of our individual lives, which seem intolerable when lived alone, become sources of healing when we live them as part of a fellowship of mutual care."

Community is like a large mosaic. Each little piece seems so insignificant. One piece is bright red, another cold blue or dull green, another warm purple, another sharp yellow, another shining gold. Some look precious, others ordinary. Some look valuable, others worthless. Some look gaudy, others delicate. We can do little with them as individual stones except compare them and judge their beauty and value. When, however, all these little stones are brought together in one big mosaic, portraying the face of Christ, who would ever question the importance of any one of them? If one of them, even the least spectacular one, is missing, the face is incomplete. Together in the one mosaic, each little stone is indispensable and makes a unique contribution to the glory of God. That's community, a fellowship of little people who together make God visible in the world.

Can You Drink the Cup?

Waiting in Community

Christian community is the place where we keep the flame of hope alive among us and take it seriously so that it can grow and become stronger in us. In this way we can live with courage, trusting that there is a spiritual power in us when we are together that allows us to live in this world without surrendering to the powerful forces constantly seducing us toward despair. That is how we dare to say that God is a God of love even when we see hatred all around us. That is why we can claim that God is a God of life even when we see death and destruction and agony all around us. We say it together. We affirm it in each other. Waiting together, nurturing what has already begun, expecting its fulfillment—that is the meaning of marriage, friendship, community, and the Christian life.

Finding My Way Home

The Attitude of Waiting

When Jesus speaks about the end of time, he speaks precisely about the importance of waiting. He says that nations will fight against nations and that there will be wars and earthquakes and misery. People will be in agony, and they will say, "The Christ is there! No, he is here!" Many will be confused and many will be deceived. But Jesus says, you must stand ready, stand awake, stay tuned to the word of God, so that you will survive all that is going to happen and be able to stand confidently (*con-fide,* with trust) in the presence of God together in community (see Matthew 24). That is the attitude of waiting that allows us to be people who can live in a very chaotic world and survive spiritually.

Finding My Way Home

Our Lives Multiply by Giving Them Away

The fruitfulness of our little life, once we recognize it and live it as the life of the Beloved, is beyond anything we can imagine. One of the greatest acts of faith is to believe that the few years we live on this earth are like a little seed planted in very rich soil. For this seed to bear fruit, it must die. We often see or feel only the dying, but the harvest will be abundant even when we ourselves are the harvesters.

How different would our life be were we truly able to trust that it multiplied in being given away! How different would our life be if we could believe that every little act of faithfulness, every gesture of love, every word of forgiveness, every little bit of joy and peace will multiply and multiply as long as there are people to receive it . . . and that—even then—there will be left-overs!

Life of the Beloved

A Prayer

Dear Lord,

Give me eyes to see and ears to hear. I know there is light in the darkness that makes everything new. I know there is new life in suffering that opens a new earth for me. I know there is a joy beyond sorrow that rejuvenates my heart. Yes, Lord, I know that you are, that you act, that you love, that you indeed are Light, Life, and Truth. People, work, plans, projects, ideas, meetings, buildings, paintings, music, and literature all can only give me real joy and peace when I can see and hear them as reflections of your presence, your glory, your kingdom.

Let me then see and hear. Let me be so taken by what you show me and by what you say to me that your vision and hearing become my guide in life and impart meaning to all my concerns.

Let me see and hear what is really real, and let me have the courage to keep unmasking the endless unrealities, which disturb my life every day. Now I see only in a mirror, but one day, O Lord, I hope to see you face to face.

Amen.

The Only Necessary Thing

DECEMBER

Radical Waiting

I have found it very important in my own life to try to let go of my wishes and instead to live in hope. I am finding that when I choose to let go of my sometimes petty and superficial wishes and trust that my life is precious and meaningful in the eyes of God, something really new, something beyond my own expectations begins to happen in me.

To wait with openness and trust is an enormously radical attitude toward life. It is choosing to hope that something is happening for us that is far beyond our own imaginings. It is giving up control over our future and letting God define our life. It is living with the conviction that God molds us in love, holds us in tenderness, and moves us away from the sources of our fear.

Our spiritual life is a life in which we wait, actively present to the moment, expecting that new things will happen to us, new things that are far beyond our own imagination or prediction. This, indeed, is a very radical stance toward life in a world preoccupied with control.

Finding My Way Home

Active Waiting

M ost of us consider waiting as something very passive, a hopeless state determined by events totally out of our hands. The bus is late? We cannot do anything about it, so we have to sit there and just wait. It is not difficult to understand the irritation people feel when somebody says, "Just wait." Words like that push us into passivity.

But there is none of this passivity in Scripture. Those who are waiting are waiting very actively. They know that what they are waiting for is growing from the ground on which they are standing. Right here is a secret for us about waiting. If we wait in the conviction that a seed has been planted and that something has already begun, it changes the way we wait. Active waiting implies being fully present to the moment with the conviction that something is happening where we are and that we want to be present to it. A waiting person is someone who is present to the moment, believing that this moment is the moment.

Finding My Way Home

God Is a God of the Present

The real enemies of our life are the "oughts" and the "ifs." They pull us backward into the unalterable past and forward into the unpredictable future. But real life takes place in the here and the now. God is a God of the present. God is always in the moment, be that moment hard or easy, joyful or painful. When Jesus spoke about God, he always spoke about God as being where and when you are. "When you see me, you see God. When you hear me, you hear God." God is not someone who was or will be, but the One who is, and who is for me in the present moment. That's why Jesus came to wipe away the burden of the past and the worries of the future. He wants us to discover God right where we are, here and now.

Here and Now

Hope

When we live with hope we do not get tangled up with concerns for how our wishes will be fulfilled. So, too, our prayers are not directed toward the gift but toward the One who gives it. Ultimately, it is not a question of having a wish come true but of expressing an unlimited faith in the giver of all good things. . . . Hope is based on the premise that the other gives only what is good. Hope includes an openness by which you wait for the promise to come through, even though you never know when, where, or how this might happen.

With Open Hands

Looking Forward by Looking Back

The expectation of Advent is anchored in the event of God's incarnation. The more I come in touch with what happened in the past, the more I come in touch with what is to come. The Gospel not only reminds me of what took place but also of what will take place. In the contemplation of Christ's first coming, I can discover the signs of his second coming. By looking back in meditation, I can look forward in expectation. By reflection, I can project; by conserving the memory of Christ's birth, I can progress to the fulfillment of his kingdom. I am struck by the fact that the prophets speaking about the future of Israel always kept reminding their people of God's great works in the past. They could look forward with confidence because they could look backward with awe to Yahweh's great deeds.

The Genesee Diary

6

Advent Attitude

I n the beginner's mind there is no thought 'I have attained something.' All self-centered thoughts limit our vast mind. When we have no thought of achievement, no thought of self, we are true beginners. Then we can really learn something. The beginner's mind is the mind of compassion. When our mind is compassionate, it is boundless."*

I like these words. Also very important for Advent. Open, free, flexible, receptive. That is the attitude that makes us ready. I realize that in Zen you are not expecting anything or anyone. Still, it seems that all the things Shunryu Suzuki tells his students are important for Christians to hear and realize. Isn't a beginner's mind, a mind without the thought "I have attained something," a mind opened for grace? Isn't that the mind of children who marvel at all they see? Isn't that the mind not filled with worries for tomorrow but alert and awake in the present moment?

The Genesee Diary

---

* Shunryu Suzuki, *Zen Mind, Beginner's Mind,* ed. Trudy Dixon (New York and Toyko: Weatherill, 1970), p. 18.

A Time for Deepening

The period before Christmas has that remarkable quality of joy that seems to touch not only Christians but all who live in our society. . . .

But Advent is not only a period of joy. It is also a time when those who are lonely feel lonelier than during other periods of the year. During this time many people try to commit suicide or are hospitalized with severe depression. Those who have hope feel much joy and desire to give. Those who have no hope feel more depressed than ever and are often thrown back on their lonely selves in despair.

When a person is surrounded by a loving, supportive community, Advent and Christmas seem pure joy. But let me not forget my lonely moments because it does not take much to make that loneliness reappear. . . . When Jesus was loneliest, he gave most. That realization should help to deepen my commitment to service and let my desire to give become independent of my actual experience of joy. Only a deepening of my life in Christ will make that possible.

The Genesee Diary

Joys Are Hidden in Sorrows!

Joys are hidden in sorrows! I know this from my own times of depression. I know it from living with people with mental handicaps. I know it from looking into the eyes of patients, and from being with the poorest of the poor. We keep forgetting this truth and become overwhelmed by our own darkness. We easily lose sight of our joys and speak of our sorrows as the only reality there is.

We need to remind each other that the cup of sorrow is also the cup of joy, that precisely what causes us sadness can become the fertile ground for gladness. Indeed, we need to be angels for each other, to give each other strength and consolation. Because only when we fully realize that the cup of life is not only a cup of sorrow but also a cup of joy will we be able to drink it.

Can You Drink the Cup?

Always Reason to Hope

I am increasingly impressed by the Christian possibility of cel-ebrating not only moments of joy but also moments of pain, thus affirming God's real presence in the thick of our lives. A true Christian always affirms life, because God is the God of life, a life stronger than death and destruction. In him we find no reason to despair. There is always reason to hope, even when our eyes are filled with tears.

Gracias!

The Hidden Way

t is hard to believe that God would reveal his divine presence to us in the self-emptying, humble way of the man from Nazareth. So much in me seeks influence, power, success, and popularity. But the way of Jesus is the way of hiddenness, powerlessness, and littleness. It does not seem a very appealing way. Yet when I enter into true, deep communion with Jesus, I will find that it is this small way that leads to real peace and joy.

The Road to Daybreak

The Christ Child Within

I think that we have hardly thought through the immense implications of the mystery of the incarnation. Where is God? God is where we are weak, vulnerable, small, and dependent. God is where the poor are, the hungry, the handicapped, the mentally ill, the elderly, the powerless. How can we come to know God when our focus is elsewhere, on success, influence, and power? I increasingly believe that our faithfulness will depend on our willingness to go where there is brokenness, loneliness, and human need. . . . Each one of us is very seriously searching to live and grow in this belief, and by friendship we can support each other. I realize that the only way for us to stay well in the midst of the many "worlds" is to stay close to the small, vulnerable child that lives in our hearts and in every other human being. Often we do not know that the Christ child is within us. When we discover him we can truly rejoice.

Sabbatical Journey

Revealing Gifts

Everyone whom I allow to touch me in my weakness and help me to be faithful to my journey to God's home will come to realize that he or she has a gift to offer that may have remained hidden for a very long time. To receive help, support, guidance, affection, and care may well be a greater call than that of giving all these things because in receiving I reveal the gift to the givers and a new life together can begin.

Walk with Jesus

God Is Faithful

The situation in our world is frightening, and many people experience deep anxieties. More than ever we will be tested in our faith. I hope and pray that the Lord will deepen our faith during these weeks of Advent and will fill us with peace and joy, which belong to his kingdom. Hope is not optimism and I pray that we all will be able to live hopefully in the midst of our apocalyptic time. We have a promise and God is faithful to his promise even when we are doubtful and fearful. As Paul says: "Our hope is not deceptive because the Holy Spirit has already been poured into us" (Romans 5:5).

Love, Henri

Joy

J oy does not come from positive predictions about the state
of the world. It does not depend on the ups and downs of
the circumstances of our lives. Joy is based on the spiritual
knowledge that, while the world in which we live is shrouded in
darkness, God has overcome the world. Jesus says it loudly and
clearly: "In the world you will have troubles, but rejoice, I have
overcome the world."

The surprise is not that, unexpectedly, things turn out better
than expected. No, the real surprise is that God's light is more
real than all the darkness, that God's truth is more powerful
than all human lies, that God's love is stronger than death.

Here and Now

Pointers to Everlasting Peace

Joyful persons do not necessarily make jokes, laugh, or even smile. They are not people with an optimistic outlook on life who always relativize the seriousness of a moment or an event. No, joyful persons see with open eyes the hard reality of human existence and at the same time are not imprisoned by it. They have no illusion about the evil powers that roam around, "looking for someone to devour" (1 Peter 5:8), but they also know that death has no final power. They suffer with those who suffer, yet they do not hold on to suffering; they point beyond it to an everlasting peace.

Lifesigns

16

Free to Love

A lot of giving and receiving has a violent quality, because the givers and receivers act more out of need than out of trust. What looks like generosity is actually manipulation, and what looks like love is really a cry for affection or support. When you know yourself as fully loved, you will be able to give according to the other's capacity to receive, and you will be able to receive according to the other's capacity to give. You will be grateful for what is given to you without clinging to it, and joyful for what you can give without bragging about it. You will be a free person, free to love.

The Inner Voice of Love

The Divine Word of Hope

The small child of Bethlehem, the unknown young man of Nazareth, the rejected preacher, the naked man on the cross, he asks for my full attention. The work of our salvation takes place in the midst of a world that continues to shout, scream, and overwhelm us with its claims and promises. But the promise is hidden in the shoot that sprouts from the stump, a shoot that hardly anyone notices.

I remember seeing a film on the human misery and devastation brought by the bomb on Hiroshima. Among all the scenes of terror and despair emerged one image of a man quietly writing a word in calligraphy. All his attention was directed to writing that one word. That image made this gruesome film a hopeful film. Isn't that what God is doing? Writing the divine word of hope in the midst of our dark world?

Gracias!

Choosing Life

In the first reading of the Eucharist today I heard: "I am offering you life or death. . . . Choose life, then, so that you and your descendants may live in the love of Yahweh, your God, obeying his voice, holding fast to him" (Deuteronomy 30:19–20).

How do I choose life? I am becoming aware that there are few moments without the opportunity to choose, since death and life are always before me. One aspect of choosing life is choosing joy. Joy is life-giving but sadness brings death. A sad heart is a heart in which something is dying. A joyful heart is a heart in which something new is being born.

I think that joy is much more than a mood. A mood invades us. We do not choose a mood. We often find ourselves in a happy or depressed mood without knowing where it comes from. The spiritual life is a life beyond moods. It is a life in which we choose joy and do not allow ourselves to become victims of passing feelings of happiness or depression.

The Road to Daybreak

Choose God's Love

Y ou must believe in the yes that comes back when you ask, "Do you love me?" You must choose this yes even though you do not experience it.

You feel overwhelmed by distractions, fantasies, the disturbing desire to throw yourself into the world of pleasure. But you know already that you will not find there an answer to your deepest question. Nor does the answer lie in rehashing old events, or in guilt or shame. All of that makes you dissipate yourself and leave the rock on which your house is built.

You have to trust the place that is solid, the place where you can say yes to God's love even when you do not feel it. . . . Keep saying, "God loves me, and God's love is enough." You have to choose the solid place over and over again and return to it after every failure.

The Inner Voice of Love

Move Toward the Light

You are constantly facing choices. The question is whether you choose for God or for your own doubting self. You know what the right choice is, but your emotions, passions, and feelings keep suggesting you choose the self-rejecting way.

The root choice is to trust at all times that God is with you and will give you what you most need. . . . God says to you, "I love you. I am with you. I want to see you come closer to me and experience the joy and peace of my presence. I want to give you a new heart and a new spirit. I want you to speak with my mouth, see with my eyes, hear with my ears, touch with my hands. All that is mine is yours. Just trust me and let me be your God."

This is the voice to listen to. And that listening requires a real choice, not just once in a while but every moment of every day and night. It is you who decides what you think, say, and do. You can think yourself into a depression, you can talk yourself into low self-esteem, you can act in a self-rejecting way. But you always have a choice to think, speak, and act in the name of God and so move toward the Light, the Truth, and the Life.

The Inner Voice of Love

Do Well the Few Things

The more I think about the human suffering in our world and my desire to offer a healing response, the more I realize how crucial it is not to allow myself to become paralyzed by feelings of impotence and guilt. More important than ever is to be very faithful to my vocation to do well the few things I am called to do and hold on to the joy and peace they bring me. I must resist the temptation to let the forces of darkness pull me into despair and make me one more of their many victims. I have to keep my eyes fixed on Jesus and on those who followed him and trust that I will know how to live out my mission to be a sign of hope in this world.

Here and Now

Trust Your Vocation

You have to start trusting your unique vocation and allow it to grow deeper and stronger in you so it can blossom in your community. . . . Look at Rembrandt and van Gogh. They trusted their vocations and did not allow anyone to lead them astray. With true Dutch stubbornness, they followed their vocations from the moment they recognized them. They didn't bend over backward to please their friends or enemies. Both ended their lives in poverty, but both left humanity with gifts that could heal the minds and hearts of many generations of people. Think of these two men and trust that you, too, have a unique vocation that is worth claiming and living out faithfully.

The Inner Voice of Love

Be Free

The great spiritual task facing me is to so fully trust that I belong to God that I can be free in the world—free to speak even when my words are not received; free to act when my actions are criticized, ridiculed, or considered useless; free also to receive love from people and to be grateful for all the signs of God's presence in the world. I am convinced that I will truly be able to love the world when I fully believe that I am loved far beyond its boundaries.

Beyond the Mirror

A Prayer

O Lord,

How hard it is to accept your way. You come to me as a small, powerless child born away from home. You live for me as a stranger in your own land. You die for me as a criminal outside the walls of the city, rejected by your own people, misunderstood by your friends, and feeling abandoned by your God.

As I prepare to celebrate your birth, I am trying to feel loved, accepted, and at home in this world, and I am trying to overcome the feelings of alienation and separation that continue to assail me. But I wonder now if my deep sense of homelessness does not bring me closer to you than my occasional feelings of belonging. Where do I truly celebrate your birth: in a cozy home or in an unfamiliar house, among welcoming friends or among unknown strangers, with feelings of well-being or with feelings of loneliness?

I do not have to run away from those experiences that are closest to yours. Just as you do not belong to this world, so I do not belong to this world. Every time I feel this way I have an occasion to be grateful and to embrace you better and taste more fully your joy and peace.

Come, Lord Jesus, and be with me where I feel poorest. I trust that this is the place where you will find your manger and bring your light. Come, Lord Jesus, come.

Amen.

The Road to Daybreak

We Are Not Alone

God came to us because he wanted to join us on the road, to listen to our story, and to help us realize that we are not walking in circles but moving toward the house of peace and joy. This is the great mystery of Christmas that continues to give us comfort and consolation: we are not alone on our journey. The God of love who gave us life sent his only Son to be with us at all times and in all places, so that we never have to feel lost in our struggles but always can trust that he walks with us.

The challenge is to let God be who he wants to be. A part of us clings to our aloneness and does not allow God to touch us where we are most in pain. Often we hide from him precisely those places in ourselves where we feel guilty, ashamed, confused, and lost. Thus we do not give him a chance to be with us where we feel most alone.

Christmas is the renewed invitation not to be afraid and to let him—whose love is greater than our own hearts and minds can comprehend—be our companion.

Gracias!

Become like a Child

The great temptation is to use our obvious failures and disappointments in our lives to convince ourselves that we are really not worth being loved. Because what do we have to show for ourselves?

But for a person of faith the opposite is true. The many failures may open that place in us where we have nothing to brag about but everything to be loved for. It is becoming a child again, a child who is loved simply for being, simply for smiling, simply for reaching out.

This is the way to spiritual maturity: to receive love as a pure, free gift.

Seeds of Hope

Blessed to Be a Blessing

It is remarkable how easy it is to bless others, to speak good things to and about them, to call forth their beauty and truth, when you yourself are in touch with your own blessedness. The blessed one always blesses. And people want to be blessed! This is so apparent wherever you go. No one is brought to life through curses, gossip, accusations, or blaming. There is so much taking place around us all the time. And it calls forth only darkness, destruction, and death. As the "blessed ones," we can walk through this world and offer blessings. It doesn't require much effort. It flows naturally from our hearts. When we hear within ourselves the voice calling us by name and blessing us, the darkness no longer distracts us. The voice that calls us the Beloved will give us words to bless others and reveal to them that they are no less blessed than we.

Life of the Beloved

Our Greatest Gift

As I grow older, I discover more and more that the greatest gift I have to offer is my own joy of living, my own inner peace, my own silence and solitude, my own sense of well-being. When I ask myself, "Who helps me the most?" I must answer, "The one who is willing to share his or her life with me."

Life of the Beloved

Born to Reconcile

I f you dare to believe that you are beloved before you are born, you may suddenly realize that your life is very, very special. You become conscious that you were sent here just for a short time, for twenty, forty, or eighty years, to discover and believe that you are a beloved child of God. The length of time doesn't matter. You are sent into this world to believe in yourself as God's chosen one and then to help your brothers and sisters know that they are also Beloved Sons and Daughters of God who belong together. You're sent into this world to be a people of reconciliation. You are sent to heal, to break down the walls between you and your neighbors, locally, nationally, and globally. Before all distinctions, the separations, and the walls built on foundations of fear, there was a unity in the mind and heart of God. Out of that unity, you are sent into this world for a little while to claim that you and every other human being belongs to the same God of Love who lives from eternity to eternity.

Finding My Way Home

Love Is Stronger Than Death

God is Spirit and the Source of all love. Our spiritual journey calls us to seek and find this living God of love in prayer, worship, spiritual reading, spiritual mentoring, compassionate service to the poor, and good friends. Let us claim the truth that we are loved and open our hearts to receive God's overflowing love poured out for us. And living fully each day let us share that love in all our wonderful and difficult relationships, responsibilities, and passages.

The seeds of death are at work in us, but love is stronger than death. Your death and mine are our final passage, our exodus to the full realization of our identity as God's beloved children and to full communion with the God of Love. Jesus walked the path ahead of us and invites us to choose the same path during our lifetime. He calls to us, "Follow me." He assures us, "Do not be afraid." This is our faith.

Finding My Way Home

Remember

Remember you are held safe. You are loved. You are protected. You are in communion with God and with those whom God has sent you. What is of God will last. It belongs to the eternal life. Choose it, and it will be yours.

The Inner Voice of Love

Acknowledgments

I would like to begin by acknowledging a large debt of gratitude to Robert Durback, editor of *Seeds of Hope: A Henri Nouwen Reader* and other anthologies of Nouwen's work. A former Trappist monk, he met and became friends with Henri Nouwen during a visit to Genesee Abbey in 1974. In making my initial selection of quotes, I used Durback's personal copies of Nouwen's books that were extensively marked up with red pen and full of annotations. Durback had a knack for finding Nouwen's most quotable passages, and I used many of them here.

I must also thank all my cheerleaders at the Henri Nouwen Legacy Trust—Karen Pascal, Judith Leckie, and Stephen Lazarus—not only for their encouragement but also the hard work of proofreading. Judith was also my companion for the difficult stage of whittling six hundred pages of potential quotes to the three hundred and sixty-six you find here. Sue Mosteller, Henri's good friend, was as ever a source of strength and inspiration.

The team at Convergent was a delight to work with. Senior Editor Gary Jansen's suggestion that editing is like "composing a symphony" was the key I needed to find the rhythm, tone, and cadence of the book. Many thanks to him and all the people at the imprint who were involved with this project.

And a final thanks to my husband, Don—first reader, ruthless editor, and best friend—for his unwavering support of all that I do.

DAY BY DAY CITATIONS

January 1, *Here and Now,* pp. 16–17; January 2, *Beyond the Mirror,* pp. 56–58; January 3, *Beloved: Henri Nouwen in Conversation,* p. 21; January 4, *Home Tonight,* p. 50; January 5, *The Inner Voice of Love,* p. 101; January 6, *Life of the Beloved,* pp. 78–79; January 7, *Compassion,* pp. 11, 13, 16; January 8, *The Return of the Prodigal Son,* pp. 100–101; January 9, *The Road to Daybreak,* pp. 73–74; January 10, *Life of the Beloved,* pp. 27–28; January 11, *The Return of the Prodigal Son,* pp. 38, 117; January 12, *The Return of the Prodigal Son,* p. 38; January 13, *Life of the Beloved,* p. 49; January 14, *The Return of the Prodigal Son,* p. 100; January 15, *The Way of the Heart,* pp. 22–23; January 16, *Clowning in Rome,* pp. 28–29; January 17, *Intimacy,* pp. 15–16; January 18, *Letters to Marc About Jesus,* p. 69; January 19, *Reaching Out,* p. 106; January 20, *Here and Now,* pp. 22–23; January 21, *Here and Now,* pp. 95–96; January 22, *The Genesee Diary,* pp. 116–117; January 23, *The Living Reminder,* p. 28; January 24, *Making All Things New,* pp. 56–57; January 25, *Lifesigns,* pp. 21, 22; January 26, *Gracias!,* pp. 49–50; January 27, *Making All Things New,* pp. 35–36; January 28, *Making All Things New,* pp. 41–43; January 29, *Life of the Beloved,* p. 39; January 30, Unpublished letter, 1983; January 31, *With Open Hands,* p. 61; February 1, *In the Name of Jesus,* pp. 15–16; February 2, *Lifesigns,* pp. 36–37; February 3, *The Inner Voice of Love,* p. 59; February 4, *The Return of the Prodigal Son,* pp. 119–120; February 5, *Life of the Beloved,* pp. 72–73; February 6, *Reaching Out,* pp. 16–17; February 7, *The Inner Voice of Love,* pp. 36–37; February 8, *Reaching Out,* p. 22; February 9, *The Wounded Healer,* p. 90; February 10, *Reaching Out,* pp. 27–28; February 11, *Letters to Marc About Jesus,* p. 54; February 12, *Love, Henri,* p. 94; February 13, *Letters to Marc About Jesus,* p. 55; February 14, *Letters to Marc About Jesus,* p. 69; February 15, *Lifesigns,* pp. 47–48; February 16, *Lifesigns,* pp. 30, 38, 39; February 17, *Reaching Out,* p. 46; February 18, *Reaching Out,* p. 51; February 19, *Reaching Out,* pp. 51, 72; February 20, *Clowning in Rome,* p. 42; February 21, *With Burning Hearts,* pp. 74–75; February 22, *Clowning in Rome,* pp. 46–47; February 23, *Here and Now,* p. 20; February 24, *Reaching Out,* p. 56; February 25, *Reaching Out,* pp. 20–21; February 26, *Life of the Beloved,* p. 30; February

27, *Here and Now*, pp. 67–68; FEBRUARY 28, excerpt from a recording of Henri Nouwen's talk "Belovedness" at the National Prayer Breakfast, Ottawa, 1991 (unpublished); FEBRUARY 29, *A Cry for Mercy*, pp. 103–104; MARCH 1, *Letters to Marc About Jesus*, pp. 5–6; MARCH 2, *Making All Things New*, pp. 45–47; MARCH 3, *Making All Things New*, pp. 57–59; MARCH 4, *Letters to Marc About Jesus*, pp. 26, 51; MARCH 5, *The Road to Daybreak*, pp. 174–175; MARCH 6, *The Inner Voice of Love*, p. 88; MARCH 7, *The Road to Daybreak*, p. 156; MARCH 8, *Sabbatical Journey*, p. 165; MARCH 9, *Sabbatical Journey*, pp. 166–167; MARCH 10, *Finding My Way Home*, pp. 117–119; MARCH 11, *Out of Solitude*, pp. 55–56; MARCH 12, *Out of Solitude*, p. 59; MARCH 13, *Letters to Marc About Jesus*, pp. 41–43; MARCH 14, *Letters to Marc About Jesus*, p. 43; MARCH 15, *Making All Things New*, pp. 50–51; MARCH 16, *Clowning in Rome*, p. 25; MARCH 17, *Clowning in Rome*, pp. 28–29; MARCH 18, Unpublished letter, 1988; MARCH 19, *The Road to Daybreak*, pp. 67–68; MARCH 20, *Love, Henri*, pp. 255–256; MARCH 21, *The Road to Daybreak*, pp. 157–158; MARCH 22, *A Cry for Mercy*, p. 56; MARCH 23, *The Living Reminder*, pp. 38–39; MARCH 24, *Finding My Way Home*, p. 49; MARCH 25, *Letters to Marc About Jesus*, p. 39; MARCH 26, *Letters to Marc About Jesus*, p. 61; MARCH 27, *Show Me the Way*, pp. 61–62; MARCH 28, *Finding My Way Home*, pp. 127–128; MARCH 29, *Finding My Way Home*, pp. 130–132; MARCH 30, *Finding My Way Home*, pp. 138–139; MARCH 31, *A Cry for Mercy*, pp. 74–75; APRIL 1, *Letters to Marc About Jesus*, p. 58; APRIL 2, *Our Greatest Gift*, pp. 100–101; APRIL 3, *Compassion*, p. 16; APRIL 4, *A Cry for Mercy*, p. 85; APRIL 5, excerpt from the lecture, "Deepening a Prayer Life," given at Scarritt-Bennett Center, February 8, 1991 (unpublished); APRIL 6, *Lifesigns*, p. 39; APRIL 7, *The Return of the Prodigal Son*, p. 101; APRIL 8, *Lifesigns*, pp. 43–44; APRIL 9, *The Inner Voice of Love*, p. 72; APRIL 10, *The Inner Voice of Love*, p. 97; APRIL 11, *The Living Reminder*, pp. 22, 25; APRIL 12, *A Cry for Mercy*, pp. 23, 102; APRIL 13, *Letters to Marc About Jesus*, p. 52; APRIL 14, *Letters to Marc About Jesus*, pp. 52–53; APRIL 15, *Reaching Out*, p. 76; APRIL 16, *Reaching Out*, p. 40 and *The Road to Daybreak*, p. 184; APRIL 17, *Letters to Marc About Jesus*, p. 68; APRIL 18, *The Way of the Heart*, pp. 76–77; APRIL 19, *The Way of the Heart*, p. 90; APRIL 20, *Reaching Out*, p. 88; APRIL 21, *The Way of the Heart*, pp. 81–82; APRIL 22, *Clowning in Rome*, pp. 100–101; APRIL 23, *Clowning in Rome*, p. 67; APRIL 24, *Out of Solitude*, pp. 21–22; APRIL 25, *Reaching Out*, pp. 90–91; APRIL 26, *Here and Now*, p. 66; APRIL 27, *With Open Hands*, pp. 121–123; APRIL 28, *Reaching Out*, pp. 105–106;

April 29, *The Genesee Diary*, p. 124; April 30, *With Open Hands*, p. 27; May 1, *With Open Hands*, p. 39; May 2, *Intimacy*, pp. 151–152; May 3, *With Open Hands*, p. 47; May 4, *The Genesee Diary*, p. 74; May 5, *The Genesee Diary*, p. 20; May 6, Unpublished letter, 1995; May 7, *The Wounded Healer*, pp. 97–98; May 8, *Reaching Out*, p. 73; May 9, *Reaching Out*, pp. 107–108; May 10, *The Genesee Diary*, p. 53; May 11, *The Genesee Diary*, p. 77; May 12, *The Genesee Diary*, p. 120; May 13, *The Living Reminder*, pp. 51–52; May 14, *Clowning in Rome*, pp. 69–70; May 15, *Clowning in Rome*, p. 76; May 16, *The Genesee Diary*, p. 170; May 17, *Gracias!*, pp. 30–31; May 18, *Letters to Marc About Jesus*, pp. 76–77; May 19, *Compassion*, pp. 108–109; May 20, *Reaching Out*, pp. 108–109; May 21, *Making All Things New*, pp. 82–83; May 22, Unpublished letter, 1982; May 23, *Making All Things New*, p. 87; May 24, *Reaching Out*, pp. 112–113; May 25, *Reaching Out*, p. 109; May 26, *Compassion*, pp. 114–115, 119; May 27, *A Cry for Mercy*, p. 109; May 28, *The Way of the Heart*, p. 69; May 29, *The Way of the Heart*, pp. 26–27; May 30, *Beloved: Henri Nouwen in Conversation*, p. 13; May 31, *With Open Hands*, p. 45; June 1, *Here and Now*, pp. 30–31; June 2, *The Return of the Prodigal Son*, p. 68; June 3, *Creative Ministry*, pp. 96–97; June 4, *Creative Ministry*, p. 96; June 5, *Lifesigns*, p. 102; June 6, *The Return of the Prodigal Son*, p. 106; June 7, *Lifesigns*, pp. 98–99; June 8, *Clowning in Rome*, pp. 26–27; June 9, *Making All Things New*, pp. 74–75; June 10, *Clowning in Rome*, pp. 30–31; June 11, *Clowning in Rome*, pp. 13–14; June 12, *Adam*, p. 37; June 13, *The Selfless Way of Christ*, p. 58; June 14, *Reaching Out*, p. 42; June 15, *The Genesee Diary*, p. 123; June 16, *The Way of the Heart*, p. 34 and *Out of Solitude*, pp. 40–41; June 17, excerpt from a recording of Henri Nouwen's talk "Caring for the Whole Person" at York Central Hospital, 1992 (unpublished); June 18, *Reaching Out*, p. 43; June 19, *The Way of the Heart*, pp. 34–35; June 20, *The Wounded Healer*, p. 52; June 21, *Here and Now*, pp. 144–145; June 22, *Out of Solitude*, pp. 42–43; June 23, *Out of Solitude*, p. 34; June 24, *Out of Solitude*, pp. 36–37; June 25, *Care and the Elderly*, p. 3; June 26, *Aging*, p. 111; June 27, *Aging*, p. 95; June 28, *Aging*, pp. 102–103; June 29, *Aging*, p. 137; June 30, *A Cry for Mercy*, pp. 45–46; July 1, *A Cry for Mercy*, p. 149; July 2, *The Return of the Prodigal Son*, p. 80; July 3, *A Cry for Mercy*, pp. 86–87; July 4, *Creative Ministry*, pp. 106–107; July 5, *Clowning in Rome*, pp. 86–87; July 6, *Clowning in Rome*, pp. 87–88; July 7, *Here and Now*, p. 195; July 8, *Clowning in Rome*, pp. 91–92; July 9, *Clowning in Rome*, pp. 92–93; July 10, *Out of Solitude*,

111; SEPTEMBER 7, *Aging,* pp. 58–59; SEPTEMBER 8, *Life of the Beloved,* pp. 96–97; SEPTEMBER 9, *Out of Solitude,* pp. 52–53; SEPTEMBER 10, *Lifesigns,* pp. 61–62; SEPTEMBER 11, *Love, Henri,* p. 222; SEPTEMBER 12, *Lifesigns,* p. 63; SEPTEMBER 13, *Lifesigns,* pp. 106, 109, 111; SEPTEMBER 14, *The Road to Daybreak,* p. 72; SEPTEMBER 15, *The Genesee Diary,* pp. 134–135; SEPTEMBER 16, *Here and Now,* p. 196; SEPTEMBER 17, *A Letter of Consolation,* pp. 29–31; SEPTEMBER 18, *Our Greatest Gift,* pp. 45–46; SEPTEMBER 19, *A Letter of Consolation,* p. 91; SEPTEMBER 20, *Gracias!,* pp. 53–54; SEPTEMBER 21, *Beyond the Mirror,* pp. 51–52; SEPTEMBER 22, *Life of the Beloved,* pp. 37–38; SEPTEMBER 23, *The Living Reminder,* pp. 39–40; SEPTEMBER 24, *Aging,* p. 86; SEPTEMBER 25, *Finding My Way Home,* pp. 144–146; SEPTEMBER 26, *The Road to Daybreak,* p. 130; SEPTEMBER 27, *Here and Now,* pp. 198–200; SEPTEMBER 28, *Our Greatest Gift,* pp. 35–36; SEPTEMBER 29, *Here and Now,* pp. 91–92; SEPTEMBER 30, *A Cry for Mercy,* p. 41; OCTOBER 1, *Our Greatest Gift,* pp. 16–17; OCTOBER 2, *Behold the Beauty of the Lord,* p. 19; OCTOBER 3, *Behold the Beauty of the Lord,* p. 27; OCTOBER 4, *The Inner Voice of Love,* p. 70; OCTOBER 5, *In the Name of Jesus,* pp. 25–26; OCTOBER 6, *The Road to Daybreak,* pp. 164–165; OCTOBER 7, *Finding My Way Home,* pp. 45–47; OCTOBER 8, *The Return of the Prodigal Son,* pp. 121–122; OCTOBER 9, *The Inner Voice of Love,* pp. 109–110; OCTOBER 10, excerpt from a recording of Henri Nouwen's talk "Life of the Spirit" at Praise and Promise, the Reformed Church of America, 1991; OCTOBER 11, *Sabbatical Journey,* p. 100; OCTOBER 12, *Life of the Beloved,* pp. 50, 51, 52; OCTOBER 13, *Here and Now,* pp. 108–109; OCTOBER 14, excerpt from *The Christ-Memory in Our Lives* (1995); OCTOBER 15, *With Burning Hearts,* pp. 36–37; OCTOBER 16, *Gracias!,* p. 31; OCTOBER 17, *Aging,* pp. 97–99; OCTOBER 18, *Life of the Beloved,* pp. 77–78; OCTOBER 19, *With Burning Hearts,* p. 35; OCTOBER 20, *Love, Henri,* p. 226; OCTOBER 21, *The Road to Daybreak,* p. 193; OCTOBER 22, *The Inner Voice of Love,* pp. 80–81; OCTOBER 23, *The Road to Daybreak,* p. 65; OCTOBER 24, *The Road to Daybreak,* pp. 65–66; OCTOBER 25, *The Road to Daybreak,* p. 68; OCTOBER 26, *Here and Now,* pp. 79, 81; OCTOBER 27, *Love, Henri,* p. 206; OCTOBER 28, *With Burning Hearts,* pp. 119–120; OCTOBER 29, *The Living Reminder,* pp. 38–39; OCTOBER 30, *Love, Henri,* pp. 19–20; OCTOBER 31, *With Open Hands,* p. 78; NOVEMBER 1, *The Genesee Diary,* p. 188; NOVEMBER 2, *In Memoriam,* p. 60; NOVEMBER 3, *The Return of the Prodigal Son,* p. 109; NOVEMBER 4, *Finding My Way Home,* pp. 139, 141–142; NOVEMBER 5, *Love, Henri,* p. 144; NOVEMBER 6, *The Inner Voice of*

Love, p. 63; November 7, *Gracias!,* pp. 74–75; November 8, *Love, Henri,* p. 95; November 9, *Finding My Way Home,* pp. 136–137; November 10, *With Burning Hearts,* pp. 28, 30–31; November 11, *The Road to Daybreak,* p. 138; November 12, *Can You Drink the Cup?,* p. 49; November 13, *The Road to Daybreak,* p. 141; November 14, *Love, Henri,* p. 87; November 15, excerpt from a recording of Henri Nouwen's talk on "Personal Growth" at the Covenant Commission Retreat, 1994 (unpublished); November 16, *Here and Now,* p. 78; November 17, *Sabbatical Journey,* p. 128; November 18, *Love, Henri,* p. 63–64; November 19, *Our Greatest Gift,* pp. 57–58, 59; November 20, *The Road to Daybreak,* pp. 29–30; November 21, *Clowning in Rome,* p. 51; November 22, *Love, Henri,* pp. 48–49; November 23, *Love, Henri,* pp. 87–88; November 24, *Can You Drink the Cup?,* pp. 95–96; November 25, *Can You Drink the Cup?,* pp. 96–97; November 26, *Can You Drink the Cup?,* pp. 57–58; November 27, *Finding My Way Home,* pp. 105–107; November 28, *Finding My Way Home,* pp. 107–108; November 29, *Life of the Beloved,* pp. 98–99; November 30, *The Only Necessary Thing,* pp. 204–205; December 1, *Finding My Way Home,* pp. 101–103; December 2, *Finding My Way Home,* pp. 98–99; December 3, *Here and Now,* p. 19; December 4, *With Open Hands,* p. 73; December 5, *The Genesee Diary,* p. 165; December 6, *The Genesee Diary,* p. 172; December 7, *The Genesee Diary,* p. 181; December 8, *Can You Drink the Cup?,* pp. 50–51; December 9, *Gracias!,* p. 179; December 10, *The Road to Daybreak,* p. 118; December 11, *Sabbatical Journey,* p. 71; December 12, *Walk with Jesus,* p. 35; December 13, *Love, Henri,* p. 44; December 14, *Here and Now,* pp. 39–40; December 15, *Lifesigns,* pp. 102–103; December 16, *The Inner Voice of Love,* p. 66; December 17, *Gracias!,* p. 62; December 18, *The Road to Daybreak,* p. 138; December 19, *The Inner Voice of Love,* p. 8; December 20, *The Inner Voice of Love,* pp. 113–114; December 21, *Here and Now,* p. 59; December 22, *The Inner Voice of Love,* pp. 32–33; December 23, *Beyond the Mirror,* p. 58; December 24, *The Road to Daybreak,* p. 102; December 25, *Gracias!,* p. 82; December 26, "Journal draft" in *Seeds of Hope,* p. 26; December 27, *Life of the Beloved,* p. 67; December 28, *Life of the Beloved,* p. 90; December 29, *Finding My Way Home,* p. 132; December 30, *Finding My Way Home,* pp. 156–157; December 31, *The Inner Voice of Love,* p. 115

WORKS CITED AND PERMISSIONS